To Preson
who is always a help
when I am anxious

Affectionately

Randolph

5/3/58

# Be Not Anxious

Peace does not mean the end of all our striving,
Joy does not mean the drying of all tears,
Peace is the power that comes to souls arriving
Up to the light where God Himself appears.

Joy is the wine that God is ever pouring
Into the hearts of those who strive with Him,
Lighting their eyes to vision and adoring,
Strength'ning their arms to warfare glad and grim.

G. A. Studdert-Kennedy


The peace of God, it is no peace,
But strife closed in the sod.
Yet, brothers, pray for but one thing—
The marvelous peace of God.

William Alexander Percy


Be not anxious about tomorrow,
Let tomorrow be anxious about itself;
Surely there are troubles enough today!

Matthew 6:34 (E)

# BE
# NOT
# ANXIOUS

---

BY RANDOLPH CRUMP MILLER

---

GREENWICH · CONNECTICUT · 1957

© 1957 by The Seabury Press, Incorporated
Library of Congress Catalog Card Number: 57-5736
Design by Stefan Salter
Printed in the United States of America

TO

ELIZABETH FOWLKES MILLER

# Preface

When Jesus said, "Be not anxious," he was pointing to a way of life. The Christian answer to anxiety is found within the community of faithful people. When you have achieved an attitude of faith in God, of commitment to Jesus as your Christ, and of response to the Holy Spirit in your life, the result will be a dynamic peace that passes understanding.

Many people who suffer from worry, frustration, loneliness, fear, and anxiety are seeking solutions to their problems. I am convinced that such answers are available and are to be found in our biblical heritage. The insights of theology and psychology are being brought together in a system of feeling, thinking, and acting that supports the unity of personality. This is accomplished within the framework of the decisions of daily living, and the gifts of God promised in the Gospel are available *now*.

The answer to your quest is not always easy to find, and it cannot be achieved in three easy lessons. The overcoming of anxiety lies primarily in the achievement of a way of life in which you live by faith and, therefore, experience the gracious love of God in your life. This does not depend primarily on what you *do,* for the beginning of Christian faith is found in an attitude whereby *you accept the fact that God accepts you as you are!* This book is a guide to you who are seeking to find the healing of your separation from God and from your fellows. You can grow into this kind of faith.

Whatever insights you may find in these pages can be traced to my own background and experience. It is difficult to list the people who should be credited as giving me these insights. But surely I learned from a mother who suffered from multiple sclerosis for almost twenty years and whose faith sustained her and kept her free from anxiety. I have learned as those I loved died from polio or cancer; as I sought to be a pastor to a congregation; as I dealt with the problems of college and seminary students; and as I rethought all of this in terms of Christian education and theology. Learning to live in a family with six children, in which a sense of the redemptive community is shared through relationships as much as through words, completes the picture.

One cannot live with books for a lifetime without great debt to many writers. Occasionally their names appear in the footnotes, but more often their ideas have become my own and I no longer remember the source.

Permission to use quotations is indicated in the footnotes. I have used abbreviations to identify twelve translations of the Bible, quotations from which have been used with the permission of the copyright owners.

RSV   *Revised Standard Version of the Bible* (copyright, 1946, 1952, by the Division of Christian Education of the National Council of Churches of Christ in the United States of America).

G   *The Complete Bible: An American Translation,* by Edgar J. Goodspeed and J. M. Powis Smith (copyright 1939 by the University of Chicago Press).

P   *The Four Gospels Translated into Modern English, The Young Church in Action,* and *Letters to Young Churches,* by J. B. Phillips (copyright, 1952, 1947, 1955, by the Macmillan Co.).

E   *What Jesus Taught,* by Burton Scott Easton (copyright 1938 by Burton Scott Easton).

VK *Berkeley Version of the New Testament,* by Gerrit Verkuyl (copyright 1945 by Gerrit Verkuyl and Zondervan Publishing House).

K *The New Testament* in the translation of Ronald A. Knox (copyright 1944 by Sheed & Ward, Inc.).

W *The New Testament in Modern Speech,* by R. F. Weymouth (Pilgrim Press and Harper & Brothers).

M *The Bible: A New Translation,* by James Moffatt (copyright 1922, 1935, and 1950 by Harper & Brothers).

20 *The Twentieth Century New Testament* (copyright 1900-1904 by the Fleming H. Revell Co.).

B *The New Testament in Basic English,* by I. A. Richards (copyright 1941 by E. P. Dutton & Co., Inc.).

KJ *The King James Version.*

PB *The Book of Common Prayer.*

RANDOLPH CRUMP MILLER

# Contents

xi

# PART I

## BE NOT ANXIOUS

# CHAPTER ONE

# Be Not Anxious

The woman was shown into the minister's office, and as she sat down she was wringing her hands. The minister did not have to encourage her to talk, for she was full of her tale. Concern about her husband, who was devoting too much time to activities outside the home, was her first complaint. She was upset about their financial situation, because there was never enough money to pay all the bills at the end of the month. Their son was receiving poor grades in school and was running with a group of undesirable friends. She was full of anxiety because this was occurring under her nose and she was powerless to stop it. What had she done to deserve all this?

As the minister asked questions, it soon became clear to him that she was not particularly anxious about either her husband or her son. The little world that had been under her domination for twenty years was beginning to collapse, and her ego was going to pieces with it. The signs that showed a deep-seated anxiety were symptoms of her own lack of resources in a crisis. She was burning up her energy in worry rather than facing her problem. Behind her husband's desire to be away from home and her son's lack of motivation in school was her attempt to control the family patterns of behavior from her own exclusive point of view.

It took some time for the minister to draw out of her enough information for him to see the picture accurately. He began by reviewing her version of the problem. And then she was led by careful questioning to doubt her own interpretation and to look for a different analysis of the situation. The difficult point in the counselling procedure came when she was faced with the decision to accept her own failure as a wife and mother as a major element in the family crisis. She desired deeply to place the blame on her husband and son, and she fought against the idea that the sense of separation and frustration was chiefly due to her own faults. She did not want to recognize the built-up resentments that had been developing over a period of years.

Whereas she had come to the minister with a conscious anxiety about her family, she now had to turn her view inward and become anxious about her own person and character. This was a difficult act, possible only because the sympathetic questioning of the minister led her in this direction without threatening her feeling that he accepted her as she was. He did not act as a judge, but led her to recall the many occasions that demonstrated her selfishness and use of authority.

Over a period of time, during which they explored the meaning of personal relationships, she saw more clearly that she had been treating her husband and son as things rather than as persons. She had been using them to attain her own ends, and the relationships between them had been in a non-personal basis. She came to the point where she could say, "I treated John as an 'it' instead of a 'thou.' " Finally came the desperate question, "How can I be changed?"

At this point, the minister brought the full resources of the Church to bear on her problem. She began to discover the resources of confession and the assurance that God forgives those who want to be changed. But she knew that this forgiveness by God would not be real until she had established a new kind of relationship in her home. The patterns of twenty years had to be broken and new patterns had to be established, and this was not an easy task. The husband and son were not eager to participate in another of her ideas, and she had to be careful not to seem to dominate as she struggled to treat them as ends in themselves.

Sources of power to make these changes in herself did not come readily. Worship, which had been a rather casual act, became a means of refreshment and of guidance. More and more she was aware that the grace of God strengthened her. The church was a means of grace after all! And for all these years it had provided a routine without much meaning. Her prayers took on a relevance that had previously been lacking.

Slowly but surely, her relations with her husband and son improved, and so did her relations with others. She was the same person, but there was something new that had been added. This change had taken place at the center of her person and she began to understand what it meant to be born again. Her feelings of anxiety about her husband and son still persisted, but she now felt that she could handle these emotions. Her sense of guilt, which had been hidden from her until she went for counsel to her minister, had at first estranged her from her family and from God, and then had been replaced by trust in God. Her feelings of loneliness were banished, even on those evenings when her husband was away, for no longer was she rejected by him or by God.

In such a situation as this, there is no guarantee that the wife will alter her personality in any radical way, but normally there will be a change of direction in her personality that will overcome her selfishness sufficiently for her to find new and deeper meanings in life. She may or may not be able to inspire her husband to spend more time at home or her son to get better grades, but at least she will learn to live with the shortcomings of all of them, and out of the change in her person will come a deeper family relationship.

## ANXIETY

*Anxiety is perfectly normal. It is a reaction to whatever threatens one's values. It is a mental or emotional uneasiness in the face of conditions that cannot easily be altered. It may refer to past, present, or future events. The cause can be confronted, but the person either does not see the issue clearly or does not see how he can straighten it out unaided. It is rooted in insecurity, misgiving, self-centeredness, worry, care, and fear.*

There are normal and natural concerns of life, and we would be fools if we did not think and plan carefully. We need to take care about our food and clothes. Healthful living involves intelligent choices about housing, weather, and safeguards against accidents. Fear of unsanitary conditions is wise. We seek guidance in the care and nurture of children, and parents should be informed about the influences of church, school, and community on their children's development. It takes longterm planning and sacrifice to prepare for a vocation, to make a marriage work, and to find the meaning of religious living.

But most of us do not stop there. We forget that worry will not add to our life or our stature, and sometimes we cannot recognize the inevitability of death. We face the normal responsibilities of life with fears that deny our maturity. Paul wrote that we should "be keener than ever to work out the salvation that God has given you with a proper sense of awe and responsibility" (Philippians 2:12, P), or "with fear and

6

trembling; for God is at work in you, both to will and to work for his good pleasure" (Philippians 2:13, RSV).

Beyond this, our normal concerns develop into anxieties. We worry unduly until we have sabotaged our health or our confidence or even the loyalty and trust of our children and friends. How easy it is to become a chronic worrier about both the essentials and the non-essentials of life! How often we magnify the possible evils facing us until we paralyze our power of action! "Don't worry at all then about tomorrow," said Jesus. "One day's trouble is enough for one day" (Matthew 6:34, P).

A high school boy went out with the crowd as usual. During the evening, the parents thought of all the things that could happen: drinking, petting, fast driving, and other forms of mischief. They knew that high school boys get into trouble, and one had been killed in an automobile accident the previous month. They also knew that if a teenager returns home and finds his parents in a lather of worry, he will discount all future guidance and warnings. In the background of their family life, however, was a mutual trust and love that demonstrated the cohesion of the relations between them. In spite of their frank recognition of the dangers involved, they had the maturity to go to bed and to sleep in the certainty that their boy could be trusted in such situations.

An operation was faced by a patient who knew very little about his condition. Fear of the unknown was combined with the expectation of pain. He went through many imaginary symptoms that were more dangerous psychologically than was his real condition physiologically. The doctor had guessed wrong on how much this particular patient needed to know in order to face his operation with confidence.

The expectation of the worst, in terms of a pessimistic

outlook, sometimes gives a cruel kind of satisfaction. Often, however, our anxiety contributes to the achievement of what was anticipated. Our worries often help to bring to fruition exactly what we feared. When we look forward to failure or loss or suffering, our mental attitude makes it impossible to achieve anything better. Unless the fear of failure is paralleled by a corresponding courage to succeed, the seeds are planted for a barren harvest.

Sights are set too low by those who are controlled by their anxieties. We become so apprehensive about obtaining something of a minor nature that we lose sight of our major goals. There are people who skimp and save, who will lower their ethical standards, who go too far into debt, or sometimes cheat and steal, in order to achieve a material possession that is the mark of a "successful" person. Our scale of values is turned around, so that we are more anxious about clothing and food and gadgets than we are about seeking the kingdom of God.

These anxieties are contagious. They are the mark of a fundamental insecurity and point to the false security of material possessions. We know neither peace of mind nor peace of soul, and we burn ourselves out on the merry-go-round of ceaseless activity. We want security and peace in the midst of a chaotic and confusing world. But we do not know how to go about it.

## THE PEACE OF GOD

Christianity offers a dynamic peace that overcomes our anxieties. It offers a life completely freed from care and worry. Although the peace that Christianity offers is foreign to the satisfactions of worldly living, it promises a high level of attainment. It releases the faithful to meaningful living and increased efficiency.

There is a paradox in this promise of peace. It is the promise of an abundant life in the midst of suffering, hardship, and trouble: those who endure despite oppression, those who mourn at unrighteousness, the gentle, those who hunger and thirst after righteousness, the merciful, the pure in heart, the peacemakers, and the persecuted. Those who have a right to suffer from a condition of anxiety, said Jesus, are precisely the ones who are promised blessedness or happiness in the kingdom of God.

The peace of God is not freedom from trouble, but it gives sufficient maturity to look trouble in the face and to remain poised and confident in the light of it.

> Be not anxious about tomorrow,
> Let tomorrow be anxious about itself;
> Surely there are troubles enough today!
> (Matthew 6:34, E)

It is a calamity that "be not anxious" was ever translated "take no thought." In 1611, "take no thought" meant "do not worry" or "be not anxious," but its meaning has changed over the years. It is obvious that we must know what our troubles are, must figure out the possibilities of success and failure, and must take steps to maintain ourselves and our families. Jesus was not advising men to avoid the normal concerns of taking thought about their health and clothing. He was saying that we must not be oversolicitous, must not place secondary things first, must not worry about small items when big problems are to be faced. Let us look at what he said:

> Be not anxious about your life,
>   What you will eat, or what you will drink;
> Nor about your body,
>   What you will put on;
> Is there not more to life than food?

9

And more to the body than clothing?
Look at the birds in the sky!
  They sow not, nor reap, nor gather into barns,
  And yet God feeds them;
Are you not worth more than they?
Who by worrying can prolong his life a single instant?
And why are you anxious about clothing?
  Look at the flowers in the field how they grow!
    They toil not, neither do they spin,
    And yet, I tell you, even Solomon in all his
      glory was not arrayed like one of these!
Therefore, if God so clothes the grass of the field,
  Which today exists, and tomorrow is cast into the oven,
Shall he not much more clothe you, O you of little faith!
Therefore be not anxious,
  Saying, 'What shall we eat?' or 'What shall we drink?'
    or 'How shall we get clothing?'
These things are the ideals of the heathen,
  But your Father knows that you need these things;
So rather seek first the kingdom of God,
  And all these things shall be given you in addition
                      (Luke 12:22-31, E)

Here is the answer to anxiety in terms of a living faith—
faith in God who does things for us. It is true that undue worry
cuts down the span of life, so that the overanxious die young.
It is a fact that those who are concerned with worldly goals
("the ideals of the heathen") do not find the blessedness that
Jesus promises. Such men seek on their own to promote a
peace of soul when there is no peace. They seek the satisfactions
of success when there are no enduring satisfactions. They put
their trust in men when men are not trustworthy. They place
their worldly possessions in barns when barns will burn. They
climb on a temporary plateau of seeming stability and discover
they have built their house on sand, and when the winds blow

and the rains come there is nothing left. They are, in fact, men of little faith.

## LOOKING TOWARD AN ANSWER

The answer is a simple one, and yet there is no easy way to the peace that passes understanding. Throughout the centuries men have been seeking a way to stability and security and happiness in many places and in differing cultures. Those who have found the answer have sometimes been among the uneducated and the lower classes, but they have also been among the cultivated and those deemed successful by worldly standards. They have often been Christians, and have always been religious.

Merely to realize that one is an anxiety-ridden person may add just one more worry to the unbearable misgivings about life that are already present. A young woman came to her minister with the avowed intention of overcoming her faithless fears and worldly anxieties, and she was convinced that if she would only cast all her care on God it would be enough. But her resolve was not sufficient, although it helped her in her knowledge of herself.

If a simple resolve to cast out worry were enough, none of us would suffer from fretful nights and irritable days, from physical ailments due to psychic causes, and from the misgiving that undermines our efficiency. We are caught up in a round of fears that cannot be excised by the surgery of confession to ourselves or others, or by resolutions to do better in the future. Our personalities are partially paralyzed by the anxieties already present, and only by help from the outside can we achieve the mental and spiritual health that overcomes our qualms about every tomorrow.

Most of us know what the answer ought to be, because we are not really devoid of faith. We believe in the God of Jesus Christ. At some point along the way, our education has included the teaching that we can be put back on the right track through faith in Christ. Perhaps we have heard of the peace that passes understanding, and we may have sensed it from time to time.

If the Christian Gospel has this promise, it is strange that we find these same fears and worries among those in the churches. This shows that a verbal profession of faith, even in terms of participation in the church's worship, has no spiritual power in itself. The prophets of old were suspicious of ceremonialism because it could hide the emptiness of going through the motions of worship without any real commitment of the personality.

In the churches we find, also, those who have learned how to be free from anxiety. The resources we need that come from outside ourselves are found in the Church and in the Gospel that is preached. The record of strange and almost miraculous recoveries of trust and of the achieving of spiritual maturity and poise is in the documents of Christian history and in the pastoral notebooks of the clergy of today. Victory is there for the asking.

One of the hymns of William Cowper tells the same story. Cowper was a melancholy person who in the depths of depression contemplated suicide. He believed that God was against him. He recovered sufficiently, under the guidance of a wise minister, to write some of the finest poetry in the English language, including sixty-eight hymns. Among them was "God moves in a mysterious way," and "O for a closer walk with God," both of which are helpful for those seeking release from anxiety. But chiefly he is helpful for his paraphrase of the "Be not anxious" passage

> Sometimes a light surprises
> The Christian while he sings;
> It is the Lord who rises
> With healing in his wings:
>
> . . . . . . . . .
>
> Set free from present sorrow,
> We cheerfully can say,
> Let the unknown tomorrow
> Bring with it what it may.

There is power in this kind of faith. As our anxieties creep up on us, their power to paralyze our actions and distort our personalities and increase our fears will be destroyed. Cowper, himself, sank back into melancholy; and we, too, will find that we cannot consistently avoid these anxieties. Yet there is the assurance of peace and blessedness as a gift of God, and we can enjoy the abundant life.

Let us make clear that Christian faith does not call one to an easy life. This must be reiterated in order that no reader may suspect that there is a kind of Utopia in which a life of ease and stability in material terms is promised. Because we are finite and God is infinite, the transcendent God is always standing over any achievement that is rightfully to our credit. Because the moral ideal is beyond the capacities of finite creatures, there is a permanent "upward look" no matter how good we may become. Because the price of all service of God involves sacrifice and thus those who follow Christ must take up their own cross, the problem is to move through tragedy to victory.

## WHERE TO START

One starting point in the overcoming of anxiety is prayer. As you read the prayer that follows, think of the ways in which it applies to your condition. Perhaps your work is happy and you sleep well, but you feel that your life is futile. Perhaps you see the blackness of the world and cannot see the light of trustworthiness in your companions. Perhaps you see the majesty of God but not, as Cowper says in another hymn, that

> Behind a frowning providence
> He hides a smiling face.

Read this prayer, then, as it speaks to your condition, and then pray it as it speaks to God.

Regard, O Lord, with thy fatherly compassion, all who are disquieted or tense, who cannot lose themselves either in happy work by day or in restful sleep by night, who looking within do not know themselves and looking to thee do not find thee. Lead them, we pray thee, out of clangor into quietude, out of futility into usefulness, out of despair into the sure serenity of truth. Teach them to believe that thou art faithful, and that thy charity hopeth all things and endureth all things; that all the darkness of the world, even the inner blackness of the soul, cannot quench one small candle of fidelity. Give them of thy perspective, thy humor, thy gift of tranquillity and poise. Be so patient with them that they may learn to be patient with themselves; so firm, that they may venture out and find pasture in the sunny fields of thy kingdom, where all who follow thy shepherding may find gladness and delight; in the Name of earth's most calm and daring Son, Word of God and Master of men, our Saviour Jesus Christ. Amen.[1]

The thesis of this book is partially expressed in this prayer by Dr. Suter, for the kind of peace we hope for determines whether or not we shall be freed from our inner tortures.

Whether we apply this to ourselves or to those whose lives are deeply entwined with ours, or to world events that we cannot directly control, the peace that passes understanding offers the clue to the meaning of our existence. We do not exist for food and clothing, for little idolatries and big successes, or even for moral crusades. In the last analysis, we exist only for God. This is what we fail either to understand or to accept, and so we burn ourselves out seeking lesser goals.

The basic theme of this book is found in two stanzas from the pen of a great twentieth-century Christian saint, Geoffrey A. Studdert-Kennedy:

> Peace does not mean the end of all our striving,
>   Joy does not mean the drying of all tears,
> Peace is the power that comes to souls arriving
>   Up to the light where God Himself appears.
>
> Joy is the wine that God is ever pouring
>   Into the hearts of those who strive with Him,
> Lighting their eyes to vision and adoring,
>   Strength'ning their arms to warfare glad and grim.[2]

CHAPTER TWO

# The Outside World

We become anxious because of our relation to the outside world. Although every worry is centered ultimately in the self, forces from beyond the self contribute mightily to our inner fears and conflicts.

There are the forces of nature over which we have little or no control: earthquakes, tornadoes, fires, and floods. There are the diseases that disable us or end our lives, of which cancer, heart disease, and tuberculosis are examples. Social and political forces turn our lives in unexpected ways and provide various degrees of uncertainty: warfare, police states, unjust courts, economic depressions, and crumbling civilizations. Religiously, our anxieties are increased by our knowledge that we are finite, and that ultimately we may cease to exist. To live in the shadow of such events means to many of us only an increase in our insecurity and fears. In the midst of such agony of the soul, we remember the words of Jesus:

> Fear not them who kill the body but cannot kill the soul;
> But fear him who can destroy both soul and body in hell.
> (Matthew 10:28, E)

This last fear is the ultimate one, for when soul and body are destroyed we are nothing.

## ANXIETY AND NATURE

If you lived in San Francisco in 1906, you would have a vivid recollection of what the combination of a shaking earth and a roaring fire can do to a city. When the city was rebuilt, much of the construction, especially of public buildings, was "earthquake proof," but private houses in San Francisco are no better built than those in other cities. Los Angeles, another earthquake area, has a rule restricting the height of its buildings. Fortunately, severe earthquakes do not occur often enough to arouse great anxiety, and only a small minority of the residents of the area have any fear of them.

If you lived in China, however, where floods are regular events, you might become a fatalist. Nothing much can be done to control the rampaging rivers and complete resignation seems to be the normal reaction. However, many dwellers in the lowlands develop a high degree of anxiety during the months when floods are likely to occur. Conditions are similar on certain portions of the Mississippi, Missouri, and Ohio rivers, and through the years there has been great anxiety; but there is a difference. Instead of resignation, attempts have been made to control the flood waters, warning systems have been constructed, escape plans have been systematized, and crops have been planted that withstand periodic floodings. The external reasons for anxiety have therefore lost most of their force.

Unless nature's catastrophes are relatively frequent, we use another system for overcoming our fears: we simply forget about the dangers and live as if they did not exist. This is normal, and it may be justified within reason. But no matter how much this false sense of security is built up, another hurricane will hit Cape Cod, another tidal wave will arise on the shores of Japan, and another eruption of a volcano will take place. Farmers in the dust bowl relax during the good years and forget that drought and dust storms will come again in the normal cycle of events.

Nature's catastrophes, although unpredictable in terms of specific dates, are part of the normal order of God's world. We do not understand why there must be such upheavals. Mature people, however, have learned to live with such occurrences, because they do not fear what can kill only the body. For mature people, the unpredictable nature of these events helps them to keep free from anxiety, but for those who are prone to anxiety, fear of the unknown increases their fears of they know not what.

## *ILLNESS*

Another set of anxieties centers in disease. The scourges of smallpox and diphtheria used to cause great mental anguish, and throughout early history we read of many plagues. Men took steps to control these diseases and today there is little anxiety about them. Knowledge of symptoms and the means of cure are the obvious ways of achieving freedom from fear of disease. Today's great killers are heart disease and cancer, and the great crippler is polio. Possibly polio is on the way out, but there is as yet no protection from cancer.

The increased knowledge of the possible symptoms of cancer and the need for early diagnosis have increased the anxiety of many people reaching the threshold of middle age. Cigarette smokers know they have a greater chance of having cancer of the lungs. Only through increased knowledge of early symptoms can steps be taken to eradicate cancer before it has progressed too far, and yet the dissemination of this knowledge increases the worry even of those who normally have no fears about their health. Combined with this knowledge is the worry that perhaps the doctors do not tell their patients the truth, and therefore even the reassurance of the doctors does not always overcome the fear that cancer is there. Some patients do not want to know the truth, and the doctors try to use the best possible means of maintaining the total health of their patients.

Many means have been used to overcome the fear of poor health. One extreme is to deny that illness is real, and although this helps the mental attitude of a person when normally he will recover without medical aid, it becomes a dangerous expedient when medical and surgical assistance is mandatory. Another way of overcoming anxiety is to have a fatalistic attitude: what will be will be, and I will meet each obstacle as it comes along. There is a degree of maturity in this point of view, but it may result in postponing medical aid or in a pessimistic attitude in a crucial illness.

The deep-lying need in the face of such anxieties about disease and health is faith. This is something that cannot be manufactured by the anxious person without God's help. Trust in the doctor, in the nurses, in the hospital care, and in the medicines is essential. This kind of faith depends on many factors. Some patients trust the means used for their cure when there is no basis in fact for such faith. Others refuse to have trust in spite of the evidence. The most helpful attitude operates within a wider perspective. The Christian outlook provides a framework of the whole of reality in which God is at work. The healing process is God's work, and the doctor and all his skills are the means of our cure. It is expressed in this prayer for others:

Almighty God, we entrust all who are dear to us to thy never-failing care and love, for this life and for the life to come; knowing that thou art doing for them better things than we can desire or pray for; through Jesus Christ our Lord. Amen.

Another prayer speaks more specifically to the healing power of God:

Almighty God our heavenly Father, we beseech thee graciously to comfort thy servant in his suffering, and to bless the means made use of for his cure. Fill his heart with confidence, that though he be sometime afraid, he yet may put his trust in thee; through Jesus Christ our Lord. Amen.[1]

In such ways as these, by God's grace our anxieties about our health are overcome. We are enabled to face the truth of our diagnosis and to cooperate confidently with the doctor.

## SOCIAL ANXIETIES

Many of our anxieties are caused primarily by what occurs in our environment. Even in times of prosperity, economic insecurity stands as a threat to many men and women. Unemployment or irregular employment is a possibility for a certain percentage of unskilled workers at all times. Men and women do get fired from their jobs. Depressions and lay-offs occur in specific industries or businesses. Strikes have a chain reaction effect on companies not directly involved in the strikes.

The stability of the economy is, of course, the obvious answer to these anxieties in so far as they are due to actual conditions. School teachers, for example, have tenure and cannot be fired except for incompetence or moral failure, and therefore they rarely develop anxiety about losing their positions. But they, like others in industry, worry about promotions, increases in salary or wages, and fairness of treatment.

At the lower levels of our economy, poverty becomes an issue when employment is fairly regular. At this point, inability to purchase many of the necessities and conveniences is combined with poor home conditions; often both parents work and the children are neglected; and conditions are rife for various kinds of delinquency and crime. Such a situation is frequently accepted with resignation, but among those with higher intelligence and driving ambition the rise of anxiety is normal.

But perhaps you are more familiar with the commuters' rat race, with the rush for the train or bus, the high pressure of work in the metropolis, the maneuvering for promotions, the involvement of the wives in business entertainment, and the impact of such pressures on family life. Some people take to this kind of life and thrive on the speed and competition, but others find that it places them in line for ulcers, heart attacks, and nervous breakdowns.

Help may come here by analogy from two sources. The best athlete is one who can keep his body sufficiently relaxed under tension, so that he is able to produce in the pinch. He is aware of the importance of the crucial situation, and he is keyed up to do his best, but he does not let his worry about failure interfere with the smoothness of his bodily action. The jazz drummer sets a fast pace for the band, but if he tightens up and loses the rhythm, the band loses its cohesiveness; the best jazz is relaxed in its tempo no matter how fast or slow the beat may be.

The Christian receives similar help. But it is not a gospel of relaxation, at least in the sense of taking it easy. It corresponds to the efficient relaxation that the athlete knows. It is the combining of all the forces of your personality to bring it to a high degree of efficiency. It builds up a tension that can be uncoiled in order to make the person go. When a watch spring is wound to its proper tension, it runs the watch at exactly the right speed. But when it is wound too tight, it breaks; and when it is run down, the watch will not run at all.

In a study of girls suffering from various degrees of anxiety, the home background was always an important factor. They had experienced rejection by one or both parents, but this rejection was never accepted as an objective fact. They confused their experience of rejection with unrealistic hopes of what the parent might become. What they carried over into their adult anxieties was the same as the attitudes developed in their unfortunate home experiences. But the girls who had been rejected, and who accepted it as a fact about which nothing could be done, did not have these anxieties. Not being loved is better than a fake love.[2]

Most homes keep up the *appearance* of acceptance of all the members of the family. Other homes have parents who *believe* they are loving their children. But if the child *feels* rejected, and at the same time *hopes* for acceptance, a conflict is established that may lead to the anxiety that can be overcome through Christian faith or to the neurotic anxiety that requires psychiatric care.

The Christian home, ideally, provides the love and acceptance that children need. They know they are loved, they live within a dependable structure, they are free to grow, and they are aware of the presence of God within the relationships of family living. The environment provides no conditions that lead to anxiety, and the children grow up in a normal way. Their natural childhood fears of the dark and of being alone are overcome as their other needs are met.

"But how can I be sure that my child feels no rejection?" a parent may ask. You cannot be sure, for in the complex environment in which our children live and in the midst of all their activities, the parent cannot keep up with his children in terms of providing for all their emotional needs. The parents may *think* they are giving them sufficient love and are providing an atmosphere of religious faith and then discover that the child has failed to see this. In large families, especially, it is easy for one child to feel the squeeze as he is caught between the older and younger children. Parents must provide love, justice, and tact in order to let each child know he is something special in their eyes.

As parents become aware of their responsibilities and of the danger of failure even when their intentions are good, they may become overanxious and oversolicitous. In their knowledge of what might happen, they become tense and exacting, overdo justice when each child needs individualized treatment, and create an atmosphere that becomes unpleasant for all the family. They read books on how to rear children and teenagers, and their children feel like creatures in a sociological laboratory.

Other parents assume that their good intentions are communicated to their children. They are unaware, therefore, that anything is wrong until they experience a barrier to communication that is typical with teenagers. New tensions develop during the "war of independence" that leads to unhappiness on both sides. No matter what the parents do, they either show too much authority or too little. Once they have been broken off, it is hard to reestablish means of communication at this point.

But some families grow together. The practice of attending church as a family, when the service is especially geared to the needs of the family, brings parents and children together when the children are still young. The class for parents that parallels the children's classes provides an opportunity for parents to see their role in terms of personal relationships, and their understanding of the meaning of the Gospel for themselves and for their children is increased. This kind of family solidarity guards against the sense of rejection on the part of the children, and the guidance for parents helps them fulfill their responsibilities as the children move into the more independent period of adolescence. Here we find the resources of the Gospel being used to get at the roots of anxiety in the home.

Anxiety arises among us when we consider the political scene. Always there is the danger that our civil and political liberties may be lost, and sometimes, when the political scene becomes complex, we would almost sell our freedom for a high degree of security. Fortunately, in the United States this has always been a temporary phase, and whenever liberty has been threatened from within forces have arisen to reassert our traditional freedoms. But there is no political necessity that people will always defend their liberties. It was not so in Germany in 1936 and 1937. Paul Tillich describes the situation as he saw it:

> First of all, a feeling of *fear* or, more exactly, of indefinite anxiety was prevailing. Not only the economic and political, but also the cultural and religious, security seemed to be lost. There was nothing on which one could build; everything was without foundation. A catastrophic breakdown was expected every moment. Consequently, a longing for security was growing in everybody. A freedom that leads to fear and anxiety has lost its value: better authority with security than freedom with fear! . . . The younger generation was tired of making decisions about everything, including their own existence.[3]

This was combined, he says, with a sense of loneliness and meaninglessness that separated each individual from his neighbor. In this despair, the people needed religion, and the traditional Christian forms seemed empty. So they turned to the quasi-religious symbols of Nazism and Fascism. "They sacrificed freedom for security, autonomy for certainty, individuality for community, and personality for an absolute symbol."[4]

Some of these factors are at work in our nation today, and when insecurity is combined with a fear of atomic warfare, the conditions are set for an American form of totalitarianism. At present, we seem to be moving toward the protection of civil liberties after a time of circumscribing these rights, for we have not lost our faith in democratic processes. But the elements of anxiety are standing by, ready to buy security by selling our freedom.

The answer to this question, complex as it is in the light of world events, is a religious one. Democracy in the American sense stands on the dignity of man as a creature of God. Only as God stands in the forefront of our thinking can this dignity of man stand against the onslaughts of various types of paganisms and totalitarianisms.

## RELIGIOUS ANXIETIES

Have you ever thought of what you would *be* if you were *not?* Or where are you when you are dead? Or what does it mean to be non-existent?

The non-religious man, who does not believe in God or immortality, knows that when he is dead his body will be returned to the elements. That is all there is to it. He is nothing.

The Christian faces the same problem. Whether he believes in evolution or the Genesis story or some other doctrine of creation, he believes that God created everything that is, out of nothing. If man was created from nothing, he will return to nothing.

Anxiety is traced to many occasions, such as we have outlined, but its real source lies in the threat that we may become nothing. God has created us and given to us space and time in which to live. Whatever is given to us can be taken away, and thus we can lose our space and time, and even our being. We know our bodies will be destroyed, but we do not know that we will see God after death. Our basic anxiety is that our existence is in the hands of another, and we can do very little about it. Of course, we can speed up the process through war, careless accidents, disregard for health, and suicide, and we can hinder the process by being careful, cautious, and *anxious*.

*Many people do not see their anxiety as fundamentally religious. They see it as due to childhood conditioning, poor environment, evil companions, the pressures of competition, the danger of war, and the complexity of daily living. They try to overcome their anxiety by dealing with the secondary causes because they do not see the primary cause. Even the non-religious person has anxiety that is religious at the source.*

Let us look at this. Here am I. But why am I here? Why should I continue to be? Can I do anything about it? I might *not be* at any moment. Because I am a creature, dependent on a Creator, my non-existence is a possibility. I am threatened, and this can throw me into despair. I can be nothing. Life can become meaningless. I can even continue to exist and be worth nothing.

Christianity has an answer to this fundamental anxiety that underlies all anxiety. Because God is my Creator and I am his creature, I know that I cannot control the future by myself; I know that all men, relying on all their creaturely resources, cannot guarantee my security. But I have faith and hope that God can do what men cannot do. He is the Creator, and the universe is his. "Have no anxiety about anything," said St. Paul, "but make all your wants known to God in prayer and entreaty, and with thanksgiving" (Philippians 4:6, G). "Throw all your anxiety upon him, for he cares for you." (I Peter 5:7, G)

Paul Tillich has worked out a series of parallels between our beliefs in God and our anxieties. When we arrive at that Christian maturity that accepts God as Creator, all-powerful, eternal, present everywhere, all-knowing, and loving, we have the means for overcoming our anxieties.

When I discover that I am a finite creature and that God is my *Creator,* I learn that I can cease to be. Therefore, as a creature I am anxious about *me!* But I also know that I am, and this gives me the *courage to be.* God is always at work as Creator, and he is at work in me. Therefore, I can find within myself, as a gift of my Creator, the power to overcome my anxiety. I can replace my fears and worries with a faith and courage that are stronger than my anxieties. But it is *not I* who do this; it is God at work within me.

When I "believe in God the Father *almighty,*" I am saying that God has all the power there is. My prayers begin with the recognition of "Almighty God." Here I find the answer to my search for the courage that conquers my anxiety. My anxiety does not disappear, but I have the courage to accept the fact that I am a creature and to live with my limitations.

When I pray to God who is *eternal,* I am saying that past, present, and future are seen by God as an eternal present. I remember the past, experience the present, and anticipate the future. I am anxious about the past that I remember, about the present that I experience, and about the future that I anticipate. Because God is eternal, all the moments of time are united in

27

eternity. I therefore hope for eternal life because I can participate in God's eternity. This gives me the courage to face the
threat of not-being.

When I find that God is *present everywhere*, I have the
courage to accept the realities of life. I can sing,

> Thou pervadest all things:
> Let thy radiant beauty
> Light mine eyes to see my duty.[5]

Because God is always present, I know there is no difference
between the holy and the profane. This gives me the courage
to accept the universe as my home when I have no home of
my own. I am not lost in space, because I know I cannot get away
from God.

When I recognize that God is *all-knowing*, my anxiety
about dark and hidden things is overcome. I know that nothing
is concealed, isolated, or disguised from him. What is hidden
within me and from me is known to God. Because God knows,
I can know if I have faith in him.

Finally, when I accept the fact that God is *love*, I am
united with him in a personal relationship. The anxiety of
separation from God is overcome because I have experienced
reunion with him. God's self-giving love is a mystery to me,
but this mystery is not a cause of anxiety. I know that God
seeks me, but that I must take the first step.

> I sought the Lord, and afterward I knew
> He moved my soul to seek him, seeking me;
> It was not I that found, O Saviour true;
> No, I was found of thee.[6]

The divine love of God is the ultimate answer to my religious
anxiety, and therefore to all my other personal, natural, and
social anxieties.[7]

In the long run, the cure of anxiety lies in the achievement of powerful attitudes strong enough to overcome the negative emotions of fear and anxiety. Only as we put first things first and seek God's kingdom will all the things we need for daily living be given to us.

# PART II

## ANXIETY AND YOUR WORLD

# CHAPTER THREE

# Sinmobile

In these next five chapters, we are going to look more closely at the symptoms of anxiety as they are indicated in the way we drive automobiles, in the manner in which we construct barriers to healthful living, in the confusion of the evil that goodness does, in the way we become depersonalized in our relationships, and in our failure to use tensions constructively. In each of these areas, we shall look for ways in which our anxieties may be decreased.

One of the most appalling of conditions in modern life is the number of injuries and deaths from automobile accidents. Bergen Evans, writing in *The Atlantic Monthly*,[1] pointed out the obvious fact that more than twice as many people have been killed in automobile accidents than in all the wars in which this nation has been engaged.

We must like automobile accidents, said Evans, or many of us would not be involved in them all the time. We regret that an accident has happened, but when we gather at a wreck we are more curious than sympathetic. Pictures of accidents increase the circulation of the newspapers, but the reaction of the public is neither increased sympathy nor improved caution; it is simply curiosity.

Safety campaigns have been less than successful. We have developed accident-proof highways, puncture-proof and blow-out-proof tires, shatter-proof glass, and crush-proof bodies; and the accident rate continues to be serious. The reason for accidents lies only occasionally in the external circumstances.

How do you account, for example, that in about twenty-seven percent of accidents between automobiles and trains it is the car that hits the train? This suggests that perhaps we should look more closely at the driver.

Evans summarizes the situation with cool precision: "The fact must be faced that the automobile is particularly conducive to the sort of behavior that causes accidents. The exhaustion that comes from driving and inhaling the car's fumes is insidious, resembling mild drunkenness rather than ordinary tiredness. The continual shock of driving in traffic frays nerves and strains tempers. The immense power obedient to the slightest pressure of the foot encourages the feeling of aggressive potency, particularly in the weak, frustrated, defeated, and in those suffering from feelings of inferiority. . . . Lolling on soft cushions, soothed by music, sweeping through space with a hypnotic hum, the very air warmed to please—how easy it is to deem oneself a God! And how terrible the wrath visited upon the impious wretch who would dare to disturb one's dreams or question one's divinity!

"It is amazing," Evans continues,

what delusions of grandeur and persecution seize otherwise sane men once they get behind a steering-wheel. Any attempt to pass them is an affront, to be resisted to the death. Any hesitation in letting *them* pass is studied insolence, justifying the use of violence. The slightest delay of others at a green light is a malicious prank; the least impatience of others at *their* delay is a violation of the Constitution. And so they go, chafing and raging until, worn out with fifty tantrums, they arrive home limp and exhausted to gather strength for the next morning's ordeal.

34

But these are the milquetoasts, and in their milder moments. More manly fellows assert themselves, show the other driver 'where to get off,' put him 'in his place,' which, often enough, is the hospital or grave. . . . The more socially conscious and energetic may undertake to educate those whom they regard as poorer drivers by shouting at them, crowding them, dazzling them by the glare of their headlights, and sometimes, heading at them with a burst of speed and swerving aside at the last moment. Or at least, one assumes, intending to swerve aside. . . . The police cannot always be sure just what a corpse's intentions were.

People collide at intersections not out of carelessness so much as out of resentment at the other fellow's daring to cross their path. Drivers get out of their lanes and race to death at the summit of hills because they are furiously determined to put an end to the 'persecution' of the cars dawdling in front of them. Autoists speed as much to save face as to save time, and frequently and literally lose both.

Perhaps you do not belong in this class of driver. But if you have any doubts, and you are a married person, read it to your spouse. You may be surprised at how many of these little defects can be pointed out to you.

Our problem in this chapter is not to find a solution to the question of why there are so many accidents. Behind the anxiety of the little man in the big car is a deeper anxiety that was described many years ago by Paul:

But if I do what I have no desire to do, then I am no longer doing it myself, but rather sin that makes itself at home in me. Consequently I discover the Law by my willingness to do what is right, while wrong suggestions crowd in. For in my inmost heart I admire God's law; but in my whole natural make-up I notice another law, battling against the principles which my reason dictates, and making me a prisoner to the law of sin that controls my bodily organs. Man of toils and troubles that I am, who will rescue me from this body doomed to death? (Romans 7:20-24, VK)

You can apply this to many drivers of automobiles, but it also tells us much about ourselves. The annoyances of the highway and boulevard and alley are similar to the everyday frictions of living with others. We are less subtle when we are protected by an automobile that weighs over a ton. We are caught without the protection of our manners. We are revealed more clearly to ourselves.

Pride often upsets our behavior on the highway and in the home; we envy our neighbor's new car as well as his recent raise; our anger blinds our sense of fair play at an intersection or in the kitchen; our dejection kills our hope and deepens our anxiety, and we compensate with bravado; our avarice makes trust difficult at a toll booth or in a restaurant; our gluttony leads us into unnecessary spending at all levels; and our lust for power makes us dictators in traffic, among our business associates, and in the home. These seven deadly sins of antiquity work themselves into all that we do. But when we recognize that they are at work in us, we resolve to reason ourselves out of the situation. We sing the hymn,

Turn back, O man, forswear thy foolish ways.

## REASON AND SIN

It is hard to realize that you cannot reason yourself out of anxiety or sin. Modern science has accomplished much, and we have built up our faith in its possibilities. Long ago the Greek philosophers wrote that if man knew what is good, he would do it. When we apply reason to the accident rate, we build super-highways and create conditions that would lower the number of accidents, *if* only people would behave. And we *do* resolve to behave. We understand the dangers of blowouts at high speeds. We know about fatigue and the hypnotism of straight roads.

Perhaps you have been involved in other reforms. We are faced with the problems of getting rid of war, of overcoming racial prejudice, of controlling the distribution of wealth, and of eliminating juvenile delinquency. *We know enough to do all these things. We have enough knowledge to make this world safe and all men free. Furthermore, reason has accomplished wonders in science, philosophy, and religion. But reason has never been enough!*

"Inwardly, I applaud God's disposition." (Romans 7:23, K) "In my own mind I am God's willing servant." (P) "For I delight in the law of God, in my inmost self." (RSV) But this is never enough.

In all of these instances, man is failing because he is seeking to save himself. Jeremiah saw this when he wrote:

> Cursed is the man who trusts in man,
> And makes flesh his arm of strength,
> His mind being turned from the Lord. . . .
> Blessed is the man who trusts in the Lord,
> To whom the Lord is his confidence.
> (Jeremiah 17:5,7, G)

Behind almost every misdeed there is anxiety. When you know yourself to be separated psychologically from someone, you are not sure how this barrier between you can be broken down. You lose your sense of security in this person's presence. When this occurs among children, they often do very silly things to attract attention, and some children make use of tantrums and other unpleasant devices in an anxious attempt to regain status in the sight of the one from whom they are separated.

When this separation is from God, there is no confidence.

We pray and say that "we have erred and strayed from thy ways like lost sheep. We have followed too much the devices and desires of our own hearts. We have offended against thy holy laws." Separation, willfulness, and law-breaking go together. When we are lost, we soon lack confidence because there is no one to whom we may turn. Yet we are lost because, like the sheep, we have followed short-range goals that seem immediately desirable, and therefore we have lost sight of the main path. Because this increases our anxiety, we offend against the law in order desperately to find a shortcut to our old trail. We begin running in circles, as does the lost boy in the woods. We have no point on our compass by which to become oriented.

Many of our actions do not seem directly willed. The sheep does not intend to become lost; he is following some rich grass. The teenager does not mean to pile up his father's car; he is simply letting the car out. The office manager does not plan to lose his temper; he just reached the end of his patience because of fatigue. The parents do not expect to scold their child; but they are anxious when they let their imaginations turn in the direction of possible dangers.

"In reality, it is not I that do these things; it is sin, which has possession of me" (Romans 7:17, G), wrote Paul. I cannot get out of this situation by the use of reason, because my deepest anxiety infects my reason. My total self is caught up in these acts. I cannot correct myself by use of the law, because I know in my mind what the law says, and I still break it. So my anxiety grows as my efforts to extricate myself become more strenuous.

## FAITH CAN DO IT

"For what the Law was unable to do," wrote Paul, "that God did by sending his own Son in the likeness of sinful flesh and on account of sin; He condemned sin in human nature so that the Law's rights might be completely met by us, who behave not in a fleshly but in a spiritual way" (Romans 8:3-4, VK).

Paul's faith rose to the heights of optimism:

> If God is for us, who can be against us? Will not he who did not spare his own Son, but gave him up for us all, with that gift give us everything? . . . Who can separate us from God's love? Can trouble or misfortune or persecution or hunger or destitution or danger or the sword? . . . For I am convinced that neither death nor life nor angels nor their hierarchies nor the present nor the future nor any supernatural forces either of height or depth will be able to separate us from the love God has shown in Christ Jesus our Lord! (Romans 8:31-32, 35, 38-39, G)

What happens when we apply this kind of optimism to automobile driving? We certainly cannot simply assume that if we know the rules of good driving we will arrive safely at our destination; and yet if we ignore our knowledge of the rules, we will be worse off. We need all the information we can obtain about driving skills, we need to practice good driving habits so that our car will be under complete control no matter what the other fellow does. We need to understand what changes in the weather do to the condition of the highway. All of these facts are helpful.

A small percentage of accidents is due to faulty brakes, poor lights, or worn-out tires. Therefore, we are responsible for having our automobile in the best possible condition.

With all this excellent knowledge and with our car in good shape, we are a somewhat safer risk on the highway than someone who is ignorant of the laws and whose car has bad brakes. But if the analysis by Bergen Evans is correct, we still need to deal with the driver. How steady is he emotionally? How does he react to alcohol? How fast is his reaction time? Does he drive when he is fatigued? How do his anxieties about other factors in his life affect his condition as he drives? Is he absent-minded? Is he a bully?

Psychologists have worked out aptitude tests for truck and bus drivers. By means of these insights, they have been able to weed out accident-prone drivers and increase dramatically the safe driving records of trucking and bus concerns. If a man has normal intelligence and adequate physical strength, he may prove to be a safe driver, but he needs also to have emotional balance and moral stamina. If a truck driver leaves for work after an argument with his wife, his chances for safe driving are decreased. If he is anxious about the next installment on a mortgage, the health of a child, or many other normal experiences of married life, he is not as good a risk as when everything is going smoothly.

This is not intended to be a treatise on automobile driving, but such a specific example makes clear that anxiety lies behind many of our difficulties. The Christian answer to anxiety is relevant to such difficulties as safe driving. It is enough here to make it clear that the "sinmobile" of our highways is a symptom in many ways of all of our sinfulness. If our automobile driving is like the other sins that Paul described, bred in the fundamental nature of ungoverned emotions, then only as our total personalities are committed to God is there hope of emancipation from our sinfulness and anxiety.

> O Christ, the Lord of hill and plain
> O'er which our traffic runs amain
> By mountain pass or valley low;
> Wherever, Lord, thy brethren go,
>   Protect them by thy guarding hand
>   From every peril on the land.[2]

# CHAPTER FOUR

# Barriers to Christian Living

In the previous chapter, we saw how our deep-seated sinfulness is illustrated by the way some people drive their automobiles. We cannot reason ourselves out of the disposition to misbehave, and this increases our anxiety, frustration, and sin. Now we turn to some more specific barriers to Christian living.

Each year, when spring cleaning times occurs, almost always there is an old closet, full of all kinds of items, covered with dust and cobwebs. This closet contains some things of real value, precious mementoes and forgotten treasures, but it also contains junk. We cannot take a broom and sweep it all out, for much of value may be lost. It takes time and care to rearrange the closet's belongings so that everything will be neat, clean, and valuable.

You may solve this problem in many ways. You may glance into the closet, close the door, and decide to wait until next year. You may impatiently put everything in the middle of the room adjoining the closet and call the Salvation Army to take the whole collection. You may start examining all the knick-knacks, read some old letters, and get lost in the details, finally either pushing everything back into the closet or throwing everything away. Taking inventory is a long process, requiring careful and mature judgment as you discard the valueless and keep the worthwhile things.

Our minds and wills are often very much like an old closet.

We are the product of our environments and cultures; we have been learning many ways of reacting since we were children; we have picked up bad habits and unpleasant behavior patterns; we have become satisfied with all the junk parked in our minds and hidden there. But there always comes a day when we have to decide what to do with our accumulated treasures and liabilities. We have to clean out the cobwebs and barriers of our own minds and wills, examining what is there.

We react to such a challenge with mixed feelings. Let's not even open the door of the closet, some will say. Let's put everything back and forget about it, others will say. While one person prizes everything in his barn, another prizes nothing. Most of our anxieties are caused by what is hidden from view in the closet of our minds. We have memories, half-forgotten as we face the problems of each new day, that serve to guide our attitudes and emotions as we move through life. All of our previous experiences are there, some pleasant, some unpleasant, and some so hidden that we cannot dig them out.

## JUNK IN A CLOSET

Instead of remembering events, however, let us look at our attitudes as we have made decisions in our daily living. In the letter to Titus, the author remembers what he was like before he was a Christian: "For we were once without understanding, disobedient, deluded, enslaved to all kinds of passions and pleasures. Our minds were full of malice and envy. Men hated us and we hated one another" (Titus 3:3, G).

I suggest that there are five piles in which you may deposit the junk you find in the closet of your own mind. You, the reader, will have to provide the details from your own experience.

The first pile of junk is those elements in the storage place of your mind that are "thoughtless," "deficient in understanding," "senseless," "foolish," or simply ignorant.[1]

This barrier to Christian living called thoughtlessness gets in the way of our relationships with others. We neglect to call back on a phone call. We leave toys around the house and someone falls over them. We push the light button when our feet are wet and risk an electric shock. This deficiency is common to us all. In its most amusing phase it may portray to us an absent-minded professor, but in its most dangerous form it may kill someone.

A little further along in this same letter to Titus, we read, "But avoid stupid controversies, genealogies, dissensions, and quarrels over the law, for they are unprofitable and futile" (Titus 3:9, RSV). God gave us what Hercule Poirot calls "the little grey cells" for the purpose of seeking truth and solving problems.

The thoughtless or senseless act increases our anxiety. We begin to worry about the person whose feelings have been hurt by our tactlessness. We become jittery as we remember yesterday's stupid controversy. Perhaps our relationship with that person is now broken, and we wonder how we can restore it. Will an apology help, or add coals to the fire? Can I bribe the person who is hurt, so he will forget about it? Or is it worth it?

We have to take this first pile of rubbish seriously, for it is part of our total personality. How can we dump all our thoughtless acts, foolish opinions, careless behavior, and wranglings with others into the trash heap? Once we have found the grace to do this, we can seek to be intelligent, thoughtful, sensible, and kind.

The second pile is a little more difficult to see clearly. It is made up of those acts, thoughts, and attitudes that comes from our "disobedience," "obstinacy," "rebelliousness," or "hardness of heart." [2] We may "understand all mysteries and all knowledge" and still be "nothing."

In each of us, we discover a great amount of self-will and self-love. It shows in the husband who never helps with the dishes, or in the child who insists on his own way by means of emotional outbursts, or in the mother who neglects her children in order to "serve the community." We show hardness of heart when confronted with the needs of friends and neighbors, and complete indifference when the person in trouble is a stranger.

Often this stubbornness and insistence on our own way reflects the obstinacy of a mule. The Bible story of men's desire to be like God is relevant here. Men built themselves a tower so that they could climb to heaven, for they wanted the knowledge given to God himself, and God destroyed their tower and scattered them and made a babble of their language, so that men could not understand each other.

Our rebellion is not simply against other men, for all men are creatures of God, and when we are separated from men we are separated from God. When we disobey God, we are guilty of treason against the heavenly King. We regret being so pigheaded and mulish, and we say that we will extricate ourselves from self-love. When we become contrite over our self-love, we may for the moment increase our anxiety, as a necessary prelude to the healing love of God's forgiveness. But usually, at this point, we fall headlong into the third pile of rubbish in the closet of our minds.

We have to look carefully in order to find this third pile, and often we cannot see it without outside help. But there is a pile of acts, thoughts, and attitudes by which we have been "deluded," "led astray," "deceived," "misled," and made "dupes of error." [3]

To some extent, we have been assisted in our delusions by others. We can take some solace in the fact that we have been misled by our wives or husbands, by our parents, by our schools, by our political leaders, and even by our churches. It gives us some satisfaction to know that although we have tried to understand ourselves, we have been misinformed.

False information is cheerfully accepted by many of us, and we make no serious attempt to correct it. Perhaps that is the basis for most of our racial prejudice, false standards of living, worship of gadgets, and wrong ideas about voting in elections. We were born that way, or started wrong, and you know what environment does to a person! We have even been misled into thinking that we do not need to brush the cobwebs from the attics and closets of our minds! Just shut the door and forget about it. The only thing that counts is how the parlor looks. We are pretty good as we are, although we are socially conditioned by our environment.

I do not think we ever need to be *that* deluded. When we are led astray, we really prefer it that way. Deep within us, buried below the conscious mind, there is a hidden desire to *deceive ourselves!* We are dupes, all right, but we are the dupes of our own self-deceptions. Pride is the deadliest of the seven deadly sins, because it works behind the scenes, hidden deeply in the closet of our minds.

When we discover how we have been deluded, the blow to our pride is sufficient to cause a protective reaction. We hope that no one else has discovered what we really are, although we now see it, so we continue to act as if we are something else than we really are, and therefore we become hypocrites.

The anxiety resulting from pride and hypocrisy is two-fold. Pride is our protection against discovering who we really are, and hypocrisy is the shell to guard us from being unmasked by the outside world. So we are anxious on both counts: We seek to assert our own competence and maturity to our own selves, and we seek to appear to the world as something we are not. It takes a strong broom and genuine determination to sweep out this pile.

The fourth pile is about as high as those of thoughtlessness, hardness of heart, and delusion. Many of our acts, thoughts, and attitudes reflect our "passions and pleasures," "lusts," "cravings," "vices," "desires and appetites." [4]

Often we believe that we are acting from a sense of duty or responsibility, and perhaps we may be right; but often we are glorying in our own pleasures. While happiness, blessedness, joy, and peace are promised when we live the abundant life in Christ, we take a hedonistic view of life. We become "slaves to passions and pleasures of all sorts" (VK).

The fundamental drives of man naturally lead to excess. We live by satisfying our appetites, but we live best by controlling our lusts. Often the dividing line is hard to see. A second piece of pie is good for a man who labors eight hours a day, but it is lust for an overweight lady. But for someone who exercises a little bit and is only a trifle overweight, is a second serving healthful or not?

Two Kinsey Reports have made public statistics about premarital sex behavior, indicating that many men and women satisfy their appetites prior to marriage. The satisfaction of one's craving at this point often leads to deep-seated anxieties later on.

Once a person gets caught up in the satisfaction of his cravings, he finds it difficult to extricate himself. It is hard for a person to refrain from smoking, eating sweets, or indulging in extra-marital love-making, once the habit has been established. The success of Alcoholics Anonymous is based on the recognition that an alcoholic does not have the strength to reform without God's help and the generous support of fellow alcoholics.

We resolve to stop satisfying our passions and cravings, but as soon as we think a vice has been eliminated it comes back to haunt us. But we know of rogues who have reformed, smokers who have stopped smoking, and drunks who never touch a drop, so in spite of our anxiety we know that even this difficult barrier to Christian living may be swept away.

There is a fifth pile that is easier to discover than our self-deceptions but as hard to get rid of as our slavery to passion. Before becoming a Christian, says the letter to Titus, we were "passing our days in malice and envy, hated by men and hating one another" (RSV).

Most of us are rightly shocked by the slaughter of men, women, and children in concentration camps. Capital punishment has been outlawed in some states. We do not crucify great men, at least literally, and we do not force a modern Socrates to drink hemlock. We are more subtle. We cut them dead on the street, undermine their influence with smear campaigns, provide gossip that catches fire and consumes the victim. Mental cruelty has become the chief cause of divorce.

Envy and jealousy and covetousness are common enough. We see these insidious attitudes wherever men are striving for promotion without regard to merit, wherever financial considerations are the only sign of success, wherever political power or social prestige is the governing factor in one's basic ambitions. Every time a neighbor buys a new gadget, it is a time for envying among some of the housewives.

Envy often has as its base a lack of the sense of security. If my neighbor's new car carries a higher degree of prestige than my old one, that is a matter of indifference to me unless I feel that his possession of this prestige threatens my own sense of security. If my own security is based on sound relationships and values, I may want a car like his, but I rejoice with him that he has one, and I do not covet it. Malice and envy are therefore lacking in this case.

As we look at the five piles of rubbish we have gathered from the closets of our minds, we hear the concluding word of the epistle to Titus: "Men hated us and we hated one another" (Titus 3:3b, G).

> O shame on us who rest content
> While lust and greed for gain
> In street and shop and tenement
> Wring gold from human pain,
> And bitter lips in blind despair
> Cry, 'Christ hath died in vain!' [5]

## A BROOM FOR YOUR CLOSET

Not any broom will sweep out the closet of your mind. The piles of junk which you have gathered are going to stay right there for you to look at, and they are going to make you uncomfortable. Any broom can be used to sweep all five piles back into the closet, but not to get them out of your house.

The junk is part of you, and the broom of your conscience is not enough. The help you receive as a Christian is described as follows:

But when the goodness and loving-kindness of God our Saviour appeared, he saved us, not because of deeds done by us in righteousness, but in virtue of his own mercy, by the washing of regeneration and renewal in the Holy Spirit, which he poured out upon us richly through Jesus Christ our Saviour, so that we might be justified by grace and become heirs in hope of eternal life. (Titus 3:4-7, RSV)

In other words, when we have found the piles of rubbish, we cannot haul them away. They stay right in our house until we call the Good Will wagon. Someone from the outside must help us.

This is the basic fact about the Christian faith. It leads us to accept the fact that we cannot overcome our sin or anxiety by our own power. We may reach the point of despair trying to help ourselves, but this is purely negative. There is no hope in recognizing that we are helpless. But Christianity says that there is help for us. There is something we can do.

As we move into a more complete understanding of the relation of Christian faith to our anxiety and to our sin, we see that Christ offers us the forgiveness that takes away the basis for our anxiety and sin. This forgiveness, operating directly through God's will and acting within the human situation in our human relations, cleans out the rubbish and makes us clean. Then we can begin to put back in place those things that are "true and pure and lovely and of good report" (Philippians 4:8), leaving room for whatever new treasures of right attitudes, thoughts, and acts God may give us.

If you have been realistic as you have read this chapter, you have begun to worry about the piles of rubbish you found in the closet of your mind. It has been a fatiguing task, and now you see more clearly what you have to do. Your anxieties that have become the source of your barriers to Christian living can be overcome. God's grace is real. God through Christ restores us to fellowship with him and with our fellows.

The carrying away of the piles of rubbish, the broom that sweeps clean, and the overcoming of the barriers to Christian living are made clear in the traditional language of Christian faith: "by the washing of regeneration and renewal in the Holy Spirit." The new man in Christ is not anxious about the morrow. He seeks to serve his Christ today.

49

# CHAPTER FIVE

# The Evil That Goodness Does

Some people do not understand why they are anxious and concerned because they are convinced that they are good and respectable. They find very few barriers to Christian living as they examine their obedience to the moral law. This goodness is real and widespread. Without it, our nation could not operate with its broad base of credit and trust in its business and social affairs.

A survey of religious thinking indicated that church members think of themselves as respectable, good, and law-abiding. Their sins are few and far between, and sometimes they wonder why the minister talks about sin so much when it does not involve them. They do not go to jail, and many of them have never received even a traffic citation. They do not beat their wives or commit adultery.

Goodness is not the private property of church people. Those who have no association with any religious group frequently show this same high concern for the moral law. Every community witnesses its leaders as they serve various humanitarian enterprises, conduct their businesses with honesty, stay within the law, and do their duty in many ways.

These good people are often bothered because Christianity is critical of such goodness. Of all the stories that Jesus told, the story of the Elder Son in the Parable of the Prodigal Son probably has upset the most people. You will recall how eminently respectable the Elder Son was. He never asked for his share of his father's fortune; he never left home; he never refused to work in his father's vineyard. His complaint about his father's treatment of the younger boy seemed to be justified, for when his wastrel brother came home with no money left, the father killed the fatted calf and had a big party with dancing and frivolity. Nothing like this had ever happened to the Elder Son, although he had been good throughout his life. He could not understand why his father treated him so badly, and he self-righteously refused to go to the party and referred to his brother as "this son of *yours*." With all his goodness, the Elder Son never saw his father's true nature, but was content to be obedient to his father's commands. Did the Elder Son get an unfair deal?

Jesus ran into the same kind of misunderstanding among the Pharisees. They were good men, the best men of their time. Many of Jesus' ethical teachings were taken directly from the Pharisees. It is even possible that Jesus received his early religious training at the hands of members of this group. They were conspicuously good men, in an era when many people ignored the Law and the Synagogue. Yet Jesus' vituperation of the Pharisees was eloquent in its condemnation of all that they stood for.

The prophets before Jesus ran into the same kind of trouble. Respectable and good priests maintained the Law of Moses and fulfilled all the details of the ritual. The prophets observed their keeping of the ceremonial law and condemned the ceremonial and all that the priests stood for. When Jesus was attacked by the good men of his time, he classified them with those who stoned the prophets.

Respectable people do not understand this attitude of Jesus. They do not understand *the evil that goodness does*. At the time of the Reformation, many of the leaders of the Roman Church were men of exemplary character, and the culture of the Middle Ages in its best aspects was a product of Western Catholicism. Luther, Calvin, Cranmer, and the other reformers attacked this system. Good men, whether Pharisees, priests, Popes, or honest secularists, have been attacked because of the evil that comes from goodness.

What, then, is wrong with goodness? Why does it fall short of the demands of God? Why are good people still filled with anxiety and fear?

## GOODNESS BECOMES EXCLUSIVE

Goodness so easily becomes exclusive. The good man gets hold of one idea and rides it to death. He becomes subject to exclusive loyalties that blind him to different and higher loyalties, and therefore he does not serve God with faith and hope.

The family is an instance of this. Loyalty to the family is good, but it may hinder loyalty to the community, to the church, and to the nation. In China, reverence for the father became a tentacle that sucked the life blood from the initiative of the next generation. Veneration of parents, and even of grandparents and great-grandparents, became so strong that social change was almost impossible.

As long as 2300 years ago, Plato saw the danger of family ties for public servants, and he suggested that rulers of the state place their children in a community that would provide for their nurture and education. The Communist experiment of communal nurseries in the 1920's was a recognition of the same danger, although of course it failed to take account of human nature. The Roman Catholic requirement of unmarried priests is another approach to this same problem. The cure in most cases is worse than the disease, but the diagnosis is accurate.

Jesus saw how competing loyalties can spoil us when he taught, "No one who loves father or mother more than he loves me is worthy of me, and no one who loves son or daughter more then he loves me is worthy of me, and no one who will not take up his cross and follow me is worthy of me" (Matthew 10: 37-38, G). Paul believed that the husband would spend too much time pleasing his wife, and the wife her husband, for marriage to be wise when the end of the age was expected. At the same time, Jesus advocated marriage and family life as the normal thing. But when a good home makes its loyalty exclusive, it can be opposed to the will of God.

Loyalty to the nation is good, too, and patriotism has great values for men. But nationalism is easily corrupted because it is a partial loyalty that men have promoted to the position of supreme loyalty. Patriotism, which is good in itself, easily gets in the way of the more significant loyalty to Almighty God. That is one reason why Jesus refused the temptation to be a political messiah. It is why Jesus made a distinction between the things that are Caesar's and the things that are God's. "For God, for country, and for Yale" is a good slogan only when the loyalties are kept in their proper order.

This same evil is evident in our loyalty to the church. Some people become so exclusive in their membership in the local congregation that they lose sight of their wider responsibility to the denomination, the National Council of Churches, the World Council of Churches, and the ecumenical movement. Good men and true become obstructionists within the movement toward church unity because they have a partial loyalty that they have made an all-embracing loyalty to ways of worship, theories of the ministry, or specific doctrines.

The Christian's loyalty to tradition is good, but the church in the name of tradition has opposed many advances of science, and even today there are those who place the formulas of the church above evolution, bacteriology, and even vivisection. The church opposed Copernicus and Galileo. Under the mask of loyalty we find such barriers to Christian living as stubbornness, pig-headedness, and exclusiveness. Because such people know they are right and good, they can afford to be intolerant of all other views.

These narrower loyalties to family, nation, and church are good. Yet we see the evil that goodness does when smaller loyalties fail to serve larger ones. Good people become anxious about their little loyalties, because no object of loyalty less than God himself is sufficient to cast out our fears and bring us into the right relationship with him.

## THE RIGIDITY OF GOODNESS

We live by forms and rituals that give meaning to our daily existence. The morning routine of the newspaper at the breakfast table, so enjoyable for husbands and obnoxious to all but the most delectable of wives, provides a structure for starting the day. We need structures for our experiences in order for them to be dependable. We have rituals in our homes, in our worship, and in our patriotic festivals, and they help us to feel secure. The priests are depicted in the Old Testament as keeping the age-old ceremonies, and the Pharisees in the New Testament as maintaining the Law of Moses. The liturgical revival in many denominations today is a symptom of this need.

The trouble is that good men do not see that forms should be changed. New revelations bring new forms and new occasions teach new duties in the on-going processes of history. Good priests are so wedded to empty forms that they stone the prophets. Good Pharisees fail to see the challenge of a new Gospel and kill the Christ. The medieval church cannot meet the needs of the rising nationalism or of the reformation of the faith and expels Luther. The King James version of the Bible is a best seller long after its accuracy as a translation is doubted. The Church of England still has its Prayer Book of 1662, unable to do anything about it through Parliament.

"There'll be some changes made," says a popular song, and the good man replies, "But I don't like it." Look at the world since the turn of the century and see the electric lights, the telephone, the automobile, the airplane, radio, television, and atomic energy come into being. Lovers of candlelight did not like the new lights, and lovers of horses did not like the horseless carriages. Christians who should have seen in these discoveries the revelation of God's truth rebelled against many of the findings of science, and evolution became a particularly sharp issue.

All these new things threaten the basis of men's goodness. Political changes are accompanied by a new structure of values, and good men tend to be conservative. After a war, a return to normalcy means turning back the clock to pre-war security.

Because there is change, with the old forms melting away, there is a gnawing sense of insecurity that hits all groups and, in particular, the middle and upper classes. The "respectable" classes are the most threatened, and therefore they are rigid in their inherited goodness.

It is just here, at the point at which change must be met with creative adaptability, that good men let us down. When we need moral guidance in order to cope with the new freedom of our teenagers, we are told that teenagers should behave according to the rules of the teenagers of the horse and buggy days. Some of us do not think this would be an improvement, but the point is that such suggestions are irrelevant.

The argument is as old as man. Is man made for the Sabbath or the Sabbath for man? The keepers of the Sabbath are good men, but they place the Sabbath above God's will that all men should be healed or cared for. They put their own needs above those of economic outcasts, and they place the onus of law-breaking on the one who seeks to serve the Lord under new circumstances. They love the Law because the Law protects them and their habits. They are good, loving, and conscientious —within limits. They have a closed rather than an open morality, and they are always willing to cast the first stone.

The rigid moralists use words such as duty, stability, private enterprise, and the American way of life, but they forget that "man shall not live by bread alone, . . . thou shalt not tempt the Lord thy God, . . . thou shalt worship the Lord thy God, and him only thou shalt serve" (Matthew 4:4,7,10, KJ), or, if they remember these words, they know how to use them in order to rule the people.

There is a certain efficiency about these law-abiding conservatives. They love order. They make their houses into model homes, with rooms in which the children are not permitted to play. Their kitchens are as effective as those in a cafeteria, and the food comes from freezers and cans. Their lives are as orderly as a schoolroom.

What underlies these orderly and rigidly directed lives? Is

the security found in such order a disguise for a hidden anxiety? Is the rigidity a denial of the flexibility of Christian love? Is this what Paul was pointing out when he wrote that we are not saved by anything that we do, lest we might boast?

The Christian faith, although it recognizes the order of the universe as evidence of the consistency of God's purpose, sees more deeply into the mystery of life. The meaning of the world turns not on the law of morality, but on a baby born in a stable —not exactly an orderly situation.

In contrast to the emphasis on rigidity and order, I like a house that can be lived in, and looks as if it has been lived in. I like a church in which the personal equation is on a higher level than the ceremonial. I like living where one can change his routine without wrecking someone's assembly line. I like anything that will cut through red tape and get to the heart of the matter. We can be dependable and loving and good because we believe in the Spirit of the living God rather than in the letter of the law. "The letter killeth, but the spirit giveth life." (II Corinthians 3:6, KJ)

Another danger of goodness is that it relies too quickly on force. The story is told by James Luther Adams of a conversation in the late 1930's with some businessmen who were complaining about the breakdown of the traditional virtues. One of them said that during a labor dispute some of his employees had impudently mentioned the higher profits of his corporation during the previous year. Another member of the group had an answer,

"Well, Hitler knew what to do with the unions."
So they moralized about unions, and another shouted,
"What this country needs is a good Vigilante Corps!"
Adams comments:

These men were not robber barons; they were church members! In fact, they had just been at church. Clearly we see here the destructive consequences of moralism. It begins with the assumption that man is made for the Sabbath, and it ends with the sentiment that some men are made for crucifixion. . . . Yet these were good men.[1]

## IS THIS GOODNESS?

Our virtues can be corrupted. Halford Luccock writes of "the seven deadly virtues." Paul lists some great virtues, such as speaking as an angel, knowing all mysteries, having great faith, giving all one's goods to feed the poor, and even giving one's body to be burned, but all of these are worth nothing unless one is motivated by love. Without love, these are *ersatz* virtues; they are not the real thing. When goodness is genuine, it does not do evil.

An exclusive and rigid goodness, based on loyalty to tradition and the law, is not enough. This phony goodness is a cover-up for lack of faith. It is an escape from our anxieties by using the aura of respectability. When the crisis comes, this kind of goodness fails and we seek Hitler's use of force or a vigilante committee.

Goodness needs to be transformed by the miraculous touch of God's grace. Then it becomes attractive and radiant and joyful. James Luther Adams puts it well:

The faith of the good man is not in his goodness; it is in the power which can transform 'goodness' into justice. This is not a power we manipulate; it is a power to which we surrender. It is not something we possess, but something that possesses us. It alone can save us from our 'virtue,' from our strength. It alone can overcome the moralism that destroys. It is the spirit of love, giving life and healing to all—even to those who do not deserve it.[2]

We begin to see more clearly the anxiety underlying *ersatz* goodness. One who manipulates his own goodness is like the Pharisee of whom Jesus spoke, who prayed,

"O God, I do thank thee that I am not like the rest of mankind, greedy, dishonest, impure, or even like that tax-collector over there. I fast twice every week; I give away a tenth-part of my income." (Luke 18:11-12, P)

Yet he knows subconsciously that "everyone who sets himself up as somebody will become a nobody, and the man who makes himself nobody will become somebody" (Luke 18:14, P), and therefore he strives to remain a "somebody" through the exclusiveness and rigidity of his interpretation of goodness.

Unless he can be challenged by the words ascribed to the Lord, "Let the one of you who has not sinned throw the first stone" (John 8:7, P), his condition is hopeless. There are "good" men who are so self-deceived that even if the Lord said this to them, they would pick up the stone and throw it at the adulterous woman. Has no respectable person ever participated in a lynching party? Were there no respectable persons at the crucifixion?

For such men there is no hope unless they begin to understand these words: "For it is by his mercy that you have been saved through faith. It is not by your own action, it is the gift of God. It has not been earned, so that no one can boast about it" (Ephesians 2:8, G). This is the heart of the matter, which all of us need to learn. We can be forced into despair as we try to earn our own salvation, but we cannot be forced into faith. Faith is our decision as we respond to God's gracious gift of restoration to fellowship with him.

> Not to oppose, but summon men
> Their truest life to find,

In love God sent his Son to save
Not to condemn mankind.

He came as Saviour to his own,
The way of love he trod;
He came to win men by good will,
For force is not of God.[3]

An early description of the Christians may be helpful as a conclusion to this chapter. "The Address to Diognetus," written probably in the third century, says that

Christians are not distinguished from the rest of mankind in country or speech or customs. For they do not live somewhere in cities of their own or use some distinctive language or practice a peculiar manner of life. . . . They take part in everything like citizens, and endure everything like aliens. . . . Like everyone else they marry, they have children, but they do not expose their infants. They set a common table, but not a common bed. . . . They obey the established laws, and in their own lives they surpass the laws. They love all men, and are persecuted by all men. . . . They are in need of all things, and they abound in all things. . . . By the Jews they are warred upon as aliens, and by the Greeks they are persecuted, and those who hate them cannot give a reason for their hostility. To put it briefly, what the soul is to the body, Christians are to the world.[4]

Contrast the evil that goodness does with those words from an early Christian writer. Living in the midst of irrational hostility, those Christians lived without anxiety and were to the world of that day as the soul is to the body. There is a life in the faith-grace relationship that brings us to our daily decisions without anxiety. This is the hope and promise of the Christian Gospel.

# CHAPTER SIX

# Anxiety and Apple Pie

Our anxieties are increased by the pressures of modern life. The growing use of automatic machinery is a symptom of the depersonalizing of our relations in our daily work. Vending machines eliminate the relationship of shopper and clerk. People are treated as things and are used for their ability to serve our needs. This depersonalizing of human relations has always existed, but the rise of the machine has made it harder to avoid.

An example of this is a pie from a modern bakery. This pie may have all the nutritious value and the flavor of a home-made pie. Indeed, one enterprising bakery used to advertise: "Pies like Mother used to make, 35 cents. Pies like Mother *tried* to make, 50 cents." The use of thermostatically controlled ovens, scientifically measured ingredients, and germ-proof pans gives a standardized pie that is wonderfully dependable, economic in lack of waste, and efficient in the use of proper fillings, with nothing left over. Sometimes this efficiency goes too far when bakers lower their standards in order to meet competition.

Mother's pies were not always measured with exactness; the oven was not always dependable; and if little Johnny knocked some dough on the floor, it was an inconvenience but not a sanitary tragedy. What Mother's pie had was this: her pie was *a product of love;* she added an extra measure of cinnamon because Daddy liked it that way; and she would take the pie out of the oven just in time to serve it piping hot for dessert. It was made with love; the hands that worked on the dough were her hands; and the pie was a work of art. It was personalized as a contribution to community life.

It is just at this point that a mechanized apple pie speaks with poignancy, for on the nice looking cellophane wrapping are the words: *No human hands have touched it.*

## GADGETS

The story of apple pie illustrates one of the dangers of modern civilization, in which mechanical routines are depersonalizing us and increasing our anxieties, because we insist on being individual persons and not cogs in a machine.

The products of our modern industrial civilization are of potential value to all of us. I am not adverse to standardized apple pies, and I rejoice in all the labor saving devices for the home. We cannot live well without the advantages of the machine age. We need the gadgets that produce leisure time. Where would we be without canned and frozen foods, mechanical refrigerators and freezers, stoves with thermostats on the ovens, fountain pens, airplanes for crop dusting, and even such tools as pliers and screw-drivers? The products of the machine age are indispensable. *There is nothing wrong with them in themselves. The machines we have created have a neutral moral and spiritual value.* Our problem is to learn to live creatively with them and to make them the servants of our personal relations.

What do we think about in the machine age? What do we

want most? Many of us think too much about the things produced by machines, and we come to believe that the right machine will solve our basic problems. Because money can buy the manufactured products that will solve (so many of us think) our basic problems, we place our chief emphasis on the accumulation of money. This is *not a new problem,* for men have always been anxious about *things,* but it takes a new form in this strange age of wonders and miracles produced by industrial magic.

The human mind is formed by what it uses, it is concerned with what it dreams about, and it becomes subservient to what it deems of chief value. The machine, which by the grace of God men created as a tool, becomes more than a tool. Men think about machines, seek machines, and love machines. The pursuit of things gets in the way of all other goals, and finally we think of vocation and friendship and marriage in terms of acquisition and prosperity.

Men need security and serenity in order to be free from worldly anxieties, and material possessions promise a spurious security that is a snare. What happens to our sense of well-being when the radio or television stops, the refrigerator breaks down, or the washing machine fails to work? We are helpless and frustrated and perplexed until it is repaired, and our gadgets have become so complex that an expert must be called. We have become more dependent on the repair man than on God!

## IMPERSONAL RELATIONS

If we are going to resolve our anxieties on the level of the standards of modern industrial society, we need two tools: *money* and *power*. With money, we may have the mechanized conveniences that we desire and keep them in running order, replacing them whenever something better appears on the market. I do not question the value of money or the desirability of gadgets. The difficulty becomes acute for us when we believe that through the ownership and control of machines we will resolve our anxieties.

When the love of money leads to the desire for ease and comfort, the result is the love of power. This is nothing new in man's history, and the misuse of power has always been a corrupting force, for men will sacrifice almost anything to achieve power over other men. Parents face this temptation in rearing their children. School teachers are tempted to misuse their authority with their pupils. Ambition is never satisfied until men are in control of some situation or organization. The larger and more important the store, factory, town, or church, the more satisfying it is to be the boss.

When the machine is dominant in a society, this love of power becomes mechanized. A man's value in his job is determined by his mechanical output, and the power of those over him is judged by the quantity produced. The job-holder's private life, spiritual concerns, ethical insights, social significance, and nature as a person are secondary to the question: *Can he produce?*

The result of this emphasis on mechanical production is that the man running the machine is treated as a *thing*. The depersonalizing forces of the mechanized world are such that his personal qualities are overlooked. The making of apple pie in terms of "no human hands have touched it" becomes a judgment on his meaning for society. He is a cog in a machine, a statistic on the labor market—and that is all.

If the laboring man seeks higher wages or better working conditions, he seeks this goal through a labor union. In this union he has the right to vote and may feel that he belongs to a group of fellow workers, but the union operates to some extent on an impersonal basis. The union in turn competes and bargains with another organization with impersonal standards. The man becomes part of an organization of things and is not treated essentially as a person. He is dependent on the depersonalizing forces of modern life for better working conditions.

When good relations are achieved between management and labor, two new factors are introduced into the situation: personal relations and ethical standards. Collective bargaining that reflects the personal hopes and demands of the workers, who are represented by bargainers who have good personal relations with management, leads to a new concern on the part of management for the personal welfare of the workers.

The depersonalizing forces reach further than the factory worker at his job. Because everyone is dependent to some degree upon the kind of economy in which the machine is dominant, the standards of our society turn in the direction of mechanical procedures.

No matter what your job may be, you are affected by the impersonal factors of modern life. Whenever you are treated as a thing rather than a person, your anxieties are fed. When you know that your value to society is judged in terms of your ability to produce, you begin to seek power and money as ends in themselves. You discover that your status does not depend on spiritual values or personal relations, and that your reputation is in terms of the power you can wield.

If you are anxious about such things, you cannot gain satisfaction in your job, in the machines that save you time and labor, in the commercial reaction readily produced for your pleasure, or in the status you may have obtained according to impersonal standards.

You may belong to many organizations, and when you attend their meetings you may be greeted with heartiness. But you do not recapture the sense of *community*. You may dream of returning to a pre-mechanical age, retiring to a farm, or going off in the woods. But you cannot turn back the clock of history, as Gandhi attempted to do when he introduced the spinning wheel as a protest against manufactured clothes. Gandhi avoided the problem by making the machine unnecessary, but we have to learn to live with the machine. Gandhi failed to see the potential blessings of the machine age, and our problem is to place the machine in the service of persons for the improvement of personal relations within a community.

## OUR PROBLEM

The problem is simple to define: it is the problem of harnessing the power of the machine age to the service of persons. The old battle of God or mammon is being fought on new terms. Men are anxious about their security, and they place their trust in things. Therefore, they treat other men as means to their own happiness.

Martin Buber, the Jewish theologian, has provided an analysis that makes this clear. He writes that there is an "I-thou" relationship and an "I-it" relationship. When we use persons and serve things, we have fallen into an "I-it" relationship, and this depersonalizes both of the participants. Many young people, for example, think of their teachers as objects of scorn; they are things to be combatted; they are not considered as persons. Many teachers feel helpless in such a situation, and their problem is to accept the pupil as he is. The teacher needs not only to imagine how the pupil feels, but he must see himself through the eyes of the pupil. An atmosphere is created in which the teacher experiences the pupil being educated. From this the teacher gains humility, a knowledge that he can do nothing more than accept the pupil as he is, and self-awareness, a knowledge of what aspect of reality he represents to his pupil. Out of this atmosphere comes a feeling of confidence on the pupil's part and resistance is overcome. He accepts his teacher as a person; he trusts the teacher because the teacher is taking part in his life, accepting him before seeking to influence him. Then the pupil learns to ask questions because he trusts his teacher as a person. The impersonal "I-it" relationship has been replaced by the "I-thou" relationship.[1]

The chief witness to the "I-thou" relationship is the Christian Church, which seeks to be a community of persons, a divine society treating each individual as a child of God. Behind the human "I-thou" relationship stands the eternal *"Thou,"* who is the Father of every person. The Church, full of sinful men with all the weaknesses of human flesh, witnesses to the evil in the world and provides the nucleus of a community in which men may shed their anxieties because they are treated as ends and not as means.

The first act of the Church in witnessing against the subjection of man to the machine is *worship.* When the body of believers worships God, there are no automatons. Each worshiper knows himself as a person, a creature of God the Creator, and he knows himself as a member of a community of persons each of whom is equally precious to God. This common worship is the powerhouse of all that the Church does, but it is a personal power that comes from the persuasive grace of God.

In church the worshiper confesses that he is a lover of things and admits that this is wrong. This does not solve his external relations in a depersonalized society, but it makes him know himself as a person who must treat others as ends in themselves. All men are equal in God's sight, not because they are flattened out in a false equality but because they are lifted up equally by the love of God for them.

## PERSONS BEFORE GOD

When Paul wrote to the Romans, he held out this ideal:

Your love must be genuine. You must hate what is wrong, and hold to what is right. Be affectionate in your love for the brotherhood, eager to show one another honor, not wanting in devotion, but on fire with the Spirit. Be happy in your hope, steadfast in time of trouble, persistent in prayer. Supply the needs of God's people, be unfailing in your hospitality. Bless your persecutors; bless them; do not curse them. Rejoice with those who rejoice; weep with those who weep. Live in harmony with one another. Do not be too ambitious, but accept humble tasks. Do not be conceited. Do not pay anyone back evil for evil. See that you are above reproach in the eyes of everyone. If possible, for your part, live peaceably with everybody. . . . Do not be conquered by evil, but conquer evil with good. (Romans 12:9-18,21, G)

This message stands in startling contrast to the popular secularism of our time. Paul did not promise great success in business, the accumulation of this world's goods, or the use of power over other men as a source of satisfaction. Genuine love is highly personal and finds its highest development in terms of service.

"You cannot serve God and money" (Matthew 6:24, G), said Jesus. He led up to this statement by saying,

But I charge you, so to use the wealth which is ever tempting to dishonesty as to win friends who, when it fails, shall welcome you to the tents that never perish. The man who is honest in a very small matter is honest in a great one also; and he who is dishonest in a very small matter is dishonest in a great one also.

If therefore you have not proved yourselves faithful in dealing with the wealth that is tainted with fraud, who will entrust to you the true good? And if you have not been faithful in dealing with that which is not your own, who will give you that which is your own?

No servant can be in bondage to two masters. For either he will hate one and love the other, or else he will cling fast to one and scorn the other. You cannot be bondservants both of God and of gold. (Luke 16:9-13, W)

When a magician named Simon saw what wonderful things the disciples were doing in the name of Jesus Christ through the laying on of hands,

he offered them money with the words,
'Give me this power too, so that if I were to put my hands on anyone he could receive the Holy Spirit.'
But Peter said to him,
'To hell with you and your money! How dare you think you could buy the gift of God? You can have no share or place in this ministry, for your heart is not honest before God. All you can do now is to repent of this wickedness of yours and pray earnestly to God that the evil intention of your heart may be forgiven. For I can see inside you, and I see a man bitter with jealousy and bound with his own sin!'
To this Simon answered,
'Please pray to the Lord for me that none of these things that you have spoken about may come upon me!' (Acts 8:18-24, P)

Jesus might have been speaking to today's lovers of power, prestige, and money when he said, "They do all their deeds to be seen of men. . . . They love the place of honor at feasts and the best seats in the synagogues, and salutations in the market place, and being called rabbi by men" (Matthew 23:5a, 6-7, RSV). "You cross land and sea to make one convert; and, when you have converted him, you make him twice as much a child of hell as yourselves." (Matthew 23:15, E) "You are like whitewashed tombs, which outwardly appear beautiful, but within are full of dead men's bones and all uncleanness. So you outwardly appear righteous to men, but within you are full of hypocrisy and iniquity." (Matthew 23:27-28, RSV)

Anxiety is the result whenever men place their faith in something that will not stand up under pressure. They appear outwardly to be happy and successful, and they may delude themselves into thinking that they are integrated and mature. Their anxiety may be hidden, and they may fight to keep it disguised from their acquaintances. What they lack is faith in the Eternal, in God, who gives us our ultimate security.

## UNFAITH AND FAITH

The decision to have faith in Christ is not easy. We need to ask ourselves,

> Now Advent of the love of Christ,
> Shall we again refuse thee,
> Till in the night of hate and war
> We perish, as we lose thee?
> From old unfaith our souls release
> To seek the kingdom of thy peace,
> By which alone we choose thee.[2]

We need to be released from *unfaith*. Unfaith is the great spiritual illness of our times, leading to the symptoms of personal and social diseases of the spirit. Unfaith is simply lack of confidence and trust in a person. Therefore, we become separated from our own kind and from God, and the resulting loneliness and spiritual isolation is hell. By withdrawing from the ways of God, we also disassociate ourselves from the sources of mental and spiritual healing. Our anxieties and fears grow when they are fed by *unfaith*.

Faith involves three things: right belief, commitment, and action. We believe in God the Father, in Jesus Christ his only Son, and in the Holy Spirit. We may not always be clear about the details of our ideas, but we know that God has made all that is, that he came in Jesus Christ to save us, and that he works through us as Spirit to restore us to fellowship with him. We do not have to be expert theologians to know that there is an "I-thou" relationship between man and God, and that in this personal relationship we have an ultimate security that overcomes our anxieties.

We commit ourselves to God. The word "faith" goes back to "tie" or "ligature." We are bound to God by our own act. We make a decision to trust in God. When we make this decision, we are making a choice in personal loyalties that may overturn our whole system of values. It takes courage to make such a commitment, but only by such a choice do men have the hope of an eternal relationship with their Creator.

Faith issues in action. It works in the midst of our common life. We use all of our faculties of insight, intelligence, and sensitivity to discover what God's will may be for us in each new situation. "Faith without works is dead." (James 2:20, KJ)

Those who have this faith seek to share it, for there is no such thing as unshared Christian faith. It is the pearl of great price for which we are willing to give anything, but unless we share it we cannot keep it. Faith evaporates when our hands clutch it. In attempting to give it away, we may get into trouble, but faith gives us the strength to persevere without anxiety.

We operate without fear and with joy, for we have "the assurance of things hoped for, the conviction of things not seen. . . . By faith, we understand that the world was created by the word of God, so that what is seen was made out of things which do not appear." (Hebrews 11:1,3, RSV)

Such faith as this enables us to stand as a person against the forces of depersonalization in modern society and to treat other individuals as persons. We understand that the "I-thou" relationship is more important than the "I-it" relationship, and therefore money and power and prestige take their proper place as tools to be used in the service of God. We cease to be anxious about the things of this world, and we use all the conveniences of modern life as tools to strengthen our relationships with persons and with God.

> From old unfaith our souls release
> To seek the kingdom of thy peace,
> By which alone we choose thee.

# CHAPTER SEVEN

# What Tensions Are For

I have never seen a tense turnip. The cauliflower responds to the sun but without any exhilaration. "Consider the lilies of the field, how they grow; they toil not, neither do they spin" (Matthew 6:28, KJ), said Jesus.

Some of us dream of a life without tensions. I have known people to envy the cow contentedly chewing its cud. There are people who think of retirement as spending their days like a great and revered old cabbage.

Tension involves a stretching and straining. There is tension in a tug of war. As both teams pull on the rope, which can be seen to quiver, one team overpowers the other. There is tension in a deer that hears a sound in the forest. Alertness is a form of tenseness and it is good.

A life without tensions is fit only for the vegetable kingdom. Tensions have the power to draw men upward and onward in life's quest for meaning and happiness. The trouble is that we cannot control the degree of tension, and there are strains and pulls that lead to disintegration. Men cannot spend their lives on the rack of torture, being pulled apart both physically and spiritually. Tensions also may lead to a paralysis of action. Monkeys in the zoo are caged, and at times the lust for

73

freedom arises. They shake the bars and cry in rage as their bodies quiver, and then they go into a corner and sulk. There is no solution for a caged animal.

Even as men cannot be contented cauliflowers in the vegetable kingdom, they also cannot stand the strains and stresses that beat down on them. They need a degree of tension if they are to climb the steep ascent of heaven, but they need some way of resolving them in order to have the power to climb.

## COSMIC TENSION

Our growing knowledge of the universe increases our anxiety about the relation of man to the vastness of creation. We do not need to be astronomers to know that man is a thin veneer on the surface of a large soulless ball. Man's size in relation to the universe is about the same as the smallest parasite in relation to man. When men see through the two-hundred-inch lens at Mount Palomar some of the mysteries of the heavens, they feel the insignificance that Robinson Jeffers expresses in his poem, *Thurso's Landing:*

> No life
> Ought to be thought important in the weave of the world;
> Whatever it may show of courage or endured pain,
> It owes no other manner of shining—in the broad gray
>     eye of the ocean, at the foot of the beauty of the
>     mountains, and skies but to bear pain. . . .
> For pleasure is too little, our inhuman God is too great,
>     and thought is too lost.[1]

This is the kind of tension that man can endure only with stubborn patience and courage. It lacks the radiance of Christian faith that sees the vast universe as the creation of a loving

God. It ends with the futility of the preacher who wrote Ecclesiastes:

> For everything there is an appointed time;
> And there is a time for every purpose under the heavens:
> A time to be born, and a time to die . . .
>
> (Ecclesiastes, 3:1-2a, G)

In his view, man and the beast have the same fate, "for everything is futility" (3:19, G). Because there is an appointed hour for everything, we can do nothing except get our timing right.

Take this same cosmic tension and see it within a Christian perspective. Men still do not control the time when they are born or die. The seasons of planting and garnering still recur. There is a cycle of life that provides our timing for us. But there is a difference. Because time is the creation of the living and eternal God, the eternal enters into time and transforms it. Seconds pass, minutes pass, hours pass, but in each second and minute and hour, the eternal is there and does not pass. My *now* is not a finite moment that is gone before I know it, never to be recaptured; my *now* has eternal significance because it is filled with the eternal meaning that God gives to it.

"The outward man does indeed suffer wear and tear," wrote Paul,

But every day the inward man receives fresh strength. These little troubles (which are really so transitory) are winning for us a permanent and glorious reward out of all proportion to our pain. For we are looking all the time not at the visible things but at the invisible. The visible things are transitory; it is the invisible things that are really permanent. (II Corinthians 4:16-18, P)

This faith is far removed from Jeffers' pessimism or the futility of the preacher in Ecclesiastes. For it reasserts our faith that this is God's world, and though we shall pass from this world, *what we do now* has eternal significance in God's sight.

## *PERSONAL TENSIONS*

Our tensions, essential as they are to keep us striving after the deeper meanings of life, often seem to conflict with each other. Instead of being an integrated personality, with the pull and strain of life drawing us toward higher goals, some of us are more complex and varied in our responses. We are more like a menagerie, with the tiger on top today and the ape tomorrow, and with the peacock and donkey taking their turns at the helm. We are something like William Ernest Henley's description of Robert Louis Stevenson:

> Buffoon and Poet, lover and sensualist,
> A deal of Ariel, just a streak of Puck,
> Much Antony, of Hamlet most of all,
> And something of a shorter catechist.[2]

The demands of society often force us into several roles. We are familiar with the hen-pecked husband who compensates by being a roaring lion in the office. We know men who practice all the techniques to win friends and influence people in order to sell goods, but who revert to a figure of unhealthy dominance in the home. We see children with their variety of standards, one for the home, another for the school room, a third for the church, and the most pressing one for the gang. The children seek a center of loyalty and are fortunate when the four sets of demands on them coincide, but often they are pulled apart by four types of tensions.

There is, of course, a legitimate variety in the way we behave. A growing person is free to strike out in more than one direction, and the complexity of a mature personality is a safeguard against the stagnation of routine. Our problem at this point is to avoid being confused by roles that emerge from our impulses and to achieve a genuine freedom that permits variety of action.

This balance is hard to maintain, because our freedom to adopt roles is limited also from the social side. Direction for activity comes from one's friends of the same age and social stratum. The goal is to get along with others, to shift one's goals to conform with the group, to do anything necessary in order to be liked. This process starts early in life and is reinforced as one grows up. These people are "other-directed" and find their chief source of direction in being liked. They can become members of the group only by conforming, and they find their acceptance by being what is expected of them.[3]

The tension between those who are pulled apart by a variety of roles and those who take any role that pleases their companions leaves little room for the individual who wants to be himself. Those who are rebuffed in their attempts to find a companionable group become lonely in the midst of the crowd and compensate for this loneliness by becoming cynical. Their creed reminds one of Samuel Hoffenstein's poem:

> The dinosaur and icthyosaur
> Are not among the things that are,
> Though once the beasts were features.
> Oh, how sad it is to contemplate
> How nature can eliminate
> Unnecessary creatures.

> Perhaps she will at last extend
> The process to another end,
> To man, and even woman;
> And turn the final hose of Fate
> And give the biologic gate
> To the obnoxious human.[4]

The tensions provided by our attempts to adjust to other

human beings often lead to such cynicism. Those whom David Riesman calls "other-directed" find a solution in being liked through conformity, thus resolving all ultimate tensions in terms of purely social categories.

## WHAT IS NEEDED

In all such situations, the tensions point in the wrong direction. The cynic who has withdrawn from society and who has no use for "the obnoxious human" is tied up with inner tensions. The outgoing person who is concerned primarily about pleasing others is pulled by a horizontal tension, but at least he has a clear picture of what is demanded of him no matter how often the goals of his group may change. The man who shifts roles is simply being pushed around by his tensions, and his state is either compensation for his anxieties or confusion as to his goals.

We have to learn to live with such tensions as these, and it is possible only if there is a point of tension between ourselves and God. The promise given us is clear:

Fear not, for I am with you;
Be not dismayed, for I am your God!
I will strengthen you, I will help you,
I will uphold you with my true right hand.
(Isaiah 40:10, G)

The tensions that lead to confusion are described in the Bible in terms of demon possession. If the demons are driven out, and if nothing replaces them, the demons will return seven-fold. If our anxiety about playing various roles is eliminated, something positive must replace it. If the anxiety hidden by our cynicism is discovered and driven out, a wholesome faith must be substituted. If our anxiety about security, partially satisfied on the social level by our conformity to the group, is seen as a temporary expedient, a genuine personal community must supersede it. Let us see how this is done.

A wholesome personality depends on its integration. Integration is a harmony of satisfying attitudes, emotions, appetites, and beliefs. The richness of this integration depends upon the level of values and the possible variety within its singleness of purpose. The purpose must be within the realm of possibility, and yet it must establish a tension between what we are now and what we hope to be. An ultimate concern must be in sight.

The first step toward achieving this goal is a frank appraisal of the self. The reason these early chapters have dealt with varieties of anxieties is to provide each reader with an opportunity to see where he fits into the picture. *We are not suffering from our acts so much as from our condition.* Anxiety is a condition of concern that has been turned inward, and in looking inward fails to find the security essential for meaningful living. Sin is a condition of separation from God and from one's fellow men. This admission of separation and of inability to restore the relationship on our own is the beginning of the Christian answer to anxiety.

The second step is to discover the resources of Christian faith. What are we promised if we make the effort to accept Christ? "Seek and ye shall find," he says. "Ask and it shall be given you." The unknown prophet of the exile summed it up:

> Seek the Lord while he may be found,
> Call upon him while he is near!
> Let the wicked forsake his way,
> And the unrighteous man his thoughts;
> And let him return to the Lord, that he
> may have pity on him,
> And to our God, for he shall abundantly pardon.
>
> (Isaiah 55:6-7, G)

This gift of a new relationship is the promise of the Gospel. God acts to restore us to fellowship with him. We who have lost contact with the ground of our being, who have become anxious because we have no ultimate security, who have no health in us because we have ignored the basis of our wholeness, are abundantly pardoned. We are accepted as we are so that we may become what we ought to be. Our contact is reestablished, our anxiety is overcome because of our deeper security, and we become whole again. "Thy faith hath made thee whole," said Jesus.

What God may do with us when we have taken the step of accepting his promises, no man may predict. We know that he restores us to fellowship, but the results in terms of specific activities cannot be seen in advance. Here is the element of risk. For when God brings us into the fellowship of the redeemed, he has a task for us. It may be generalized as the obedience that results from our faith, but the specific call of the individual is unique.

Some people want a warranty in advance. One man wants a promise that God will let him give up his job, because it is unpleasant. Another hopes that God will call him to the ministry, and perhaps secretly he hopes to become a bishop. Another hopes that God will permit him to keep his present high salary, even though he knows that his work is against the public interest. Even while we are seeking the Lord while he may be found, we want to *bargain with God*. But the only bargain we make is with the Devil, and so our anxieties are increased, and the state we are in is worse than before.

When you are a member of a family, you do not say, "I will be a member of this family on my own terms," for then you spoil the relationship. You ask, "What can I do for the good of the family?" You seek out the tasks that need to be done and see that these things are accomplished. The children's tasks are outlined by the parents, who supervise their work, which is in keeping with their ages and responsibilities. Parental love provides the guidance, and this love accepts the children even when they fail, as they so often do, at their appointed tasks. But the security of love and the promise of reconciliation accompany the children as they fill their unique functions as members of the family.

God's love is something like this. We call God our Father because his love parallels the parental love of our childhood experience. We are God's children, and he seeks to keep us in the right relationship with him. He accepts us even when we reject him. But we have the freedom to refuse his love, and this sets up a barrier that God overcomes when we have faith.

How much more is man worth than the birds and the flowers and the revered old cabbage! Man is not meant for the vegetable kingdom, and he can rise above the animal kingdom to the kingdom of God! Our cosmic tensions are overcome when we discover the majesty of God in and beyond the starry spaces of the sky. As man's control of atomic energy grows beyond the imagination of all save the scientists, we know that God is much greater.

The tensions of living, that seem to pull us apart, are restored to the pattern of wholeness by God's grace. God is available and we may seek the Lord while he may be found. We can take specific steps now to come into the right relationship with him, as we see clearly who we are and where we stand.

> Strange prayers ascending up to God
> Through all the aching aeons, year on year;
> Strange tongues uplifting from the sod
> The old antiphony of hope and fear:
> Strange if he should not hear![5]

# PART III

# JOY AND FAITH
# IN AN ANXIOUS WORLD

---

# CHAPTER EIGHT

# Great Christians Are Made

This and the following chapters deal with individuals who have found joy and faith in the world. Some of them lived in ages past and some are living today. Some are famous and some you have never heard of. You will be helped by them, even if you never expect to compose a cantata, write hymns or poetry, or cut hair.

Will Rogers once was asked, "What's wrong with the world?" And he replied, "I dunno; I guess it's the people." And by "people" he did not mean the criminals and the crooked rulers and the unscrupulous seekers after easy money. He meant that most folk receive just about what they deserve. Our society is made up of people.

The people include heroes who make the headlines and the undistinguished ones who work behind the scenes to make possible the work of the star. Every Sherlock Holmes has his Watson. Every star halfback has his blocking back and running guard. Daniel Webster once said that an old aunt living in New Hampshire was the strongest argument in favor of Christianity that he knew of. Even the work of Jesus might not have captured the imagination of the Palestinian, Greek, and Roman world without the support of a group of nondescript fishermen and tax collectors.

## PAUL AND BARNABAS

We know more about Paul than we do about Barnabas. Paul was an example of what a missionary ought to be, and he was the key figure in carrying the Gospel to the non-Jews. We know that he overcame strong anti-Christian tendencies and that he was made into a great Christian as a result of a conversion experience that he did not seek. Behind the story of Paul's greatness was the influence of Barnabas.

When Paul made his first visit to Jerusalem after his conversion, the leaders of the Church were suspicious of him. They knew his record as a persecutor of the Christians and they suspected a trick. Barnabas was sensitive to the genuineness of Paul's purpose and vouched for him. Later on, Barnabas sought out Paul at his home and asked him to preach in Antioch, thus instigating the widening influence of Paul's missionary work. Barnabas was the leader of the first missionary tour that left Antioch. When Paul and Mark split up, Barnabas used his influence to help Mark recover his confidence.

Barnabas gave up the leadership of the church in Antioch in order to carry on the missionary work to the heathen. He was a developer of men, and in his handling of Mark we see the Gospel providing a second chance for a man who seemed a failure. He saw the best in Paul, but in Mark he saw something more: he saw possibilities that neither Paul nor Mark himself were aware of, and he helped Mark to overcome his failure and to grow as a follower of Peter and as the writer of the Gospel.

Barnabas was a channel through whom God's grace worked. Our relationships with God are healed through the ministry of men. God acted directly on Paul at his conversion, but it was

Barnabas who served as the agent to bring Paul to the fulfillment of his destiny. This is the way God works in our world, for our personal relations in the community of faithful people strengthen us for the task that is ahead of us.[1]

## ALEXANDER CUMMINS

We all like a fighter. A minister spent his whole pastorate in Poughkeepsie. He had a reputation as a supporter of the Protestant emphasis in the Protestant Episcopal Church, and he disliked any imitation of what seemed to him Roman ceremonial. He pricked the bubbles in the pomposity of his fellow clergymen and of bishops. He attacked reactionary theology with piercing criticism. He was a relentless protagonist, and he edited a monthly journal to propagate his views.

When Alexander Cummins died, his friends remembered him primarily for his generosity and kindness. Storekeepers, city officials, garage men, clergy of other denominations, and the porter on the train agreed with the first sentence of an editorial in the newspaper: "Make no mistake—this was no small man who died in our community yesterday morning." One of his friends summed up his opinion: "Dear old Alec was one of the best men that ever lived: kind, generous, outspoken, loyal to his friends, a devout and loyal churchman who detested insincerity and doubletalk. There was never any twaddle of make-believe about him—all wool and a hundred inches wide, a most jolly, courageous, and valiant Christian gentleman."

Here we see the strain of prophetic religion, standing immovable against what seemed wrong, objecting to cant in a cantankerous manner, insisting on the truth as both a revelation from God and a discovery by men. He combined the rapier of his wit with the broadsword of his criticism to attack whatever was in the way of Christian faith, especially when he saw these obstructions within the Church itself.

High courage as exemplified in Alexander Cummins is the product of faith. He had sufficient maturity to stand his ground and to oppose, in the name of truth as he saw it, innovations that denied the faith. Often he spoke in the name of the traditions of the Reformation, but his objections were to medieval corruptions of the faith and not to new insights of contemporary knowledge.

## JOHANN SEBASTIAN BACH

It is difficult for many of us to realize that Bach was an organist and choirmaster in an obscure German church, and that his musical compositions were forgotten for a hundred years after his death.

He lived simply with a large family. Some of his sons were composers, and at least one was for many years more famous than he. He was deeply steeped in Lutheran theology and the Bible, and his music expresses the great insights of Christian faith.

He used to initial his manuscripts, "J.J." (*Jesu Juva*—Help me, Jesus!) at the beginning, and "S.D.G." (*Soli Deo Gloria*—To God alone be praise!) at the end. Music was always an act of worship to him. Albert Schweitzer writes of Bach,

This robust man, who seems to be in the thick of life with his family and his work, and whose mouth seems to express something like comfortable joy in life, was inwardly dead to the world. His religion transfigured his life, and left him tranquil and serene.[2]

At one time Bach composed one cantata a month; he wrote over three hundred of them altogether, and each one lasts about thirty minutes. They can be understood only as we pay attention to the words, for Bach combined words and music in his magnificient settings. This was particularly true of his great *Passion According to St. Matthew,* for he knew the Gospel so well that just the right words and forms were used throughout. His *Christmas Cantata,* a composition that takes over two hours to perform, catches the deep theological meaning of the nativity stories and anticipates the passion theme. Perhaps his great musical genius reached its high point with the *Mass in B Minor,* which is too elaborate for church use but which brings to the listener the profoundest meanings of the Holy Communion.

"The Devil cannot bear singing," said Martin Luther. An obscure organist of two centuries ago makes this clear. This great musical gift to the world came from a man who was "tranquil and serene." Bach lived in the world, not hungry for worldly renown, but full of faith in the Christ who makes men free. In the midst of over twenty children, he hardly had tranquility in his home, and it was a time of tension in the German nation. "Look at the head" of Bach, wrote Wagner,

hidden in its absurd French full-bottomed wig, a miserable cantor and organist in little Thuringian towns whose names we hardly now know, wearing himself out in poor situations, always so little considered that it needed a whole century after his death to rescue his works from oblivion.[3]

The secret of Bach's tranquility was not in his music, although his music was an undying expression of his faith. He had learned well Luther's words:

From faith flow forth love and joy in the Lord, and from love a joyful, willing and free mind that serves one's neighbor willingly and takes no account of gratitude and ingratitude, of praise or blame, of gain or loss.[4]

## WILLIAM TEMPLE

William Temple died in 1944. Like his father before him, he was Archbishop of Canterbury, but that was among the least of his claims to fame. He combined many aspects of sainthood with a career that seemed without strain or danger. As a boy, he was an outstanding student and an adequate athlete. He became successively a tutor at Oxford, the headmaster of Repton, rector of a parish, canon of Westminster, Bishop of Manchester, Archbishop of York, and Archbishop of Canterbury.

At an early age Temple showed great skill as a leader. In 1928, at the meeting of the International Missionary Conference, one of the committees, of which Temple was a member, found that it could come to no agreement. Temple turned the tide by bringing in a report that was sufficiently comprehensive to satisfy the warring factions.

His friend, William Paton, summarized Temple's personality as follows:

> It is not only that no one can help liking him. It is not merely that he is a consummate chairman, graceful, decisive, clear, considerate; it is not only that he can record the proceedings at the same time as he controls them and can produce, while a discussion is going on, a summary of it, thus putting secretaries to shame, *his universal acceptability as a chairman is really due to his own humility so that every one instinctively feels safe in his hands.*[5]

Because Temple was trusted, he could afford to take risks. He was outspoken on social and theological questions. He was listened to by the politicians as they considered the social issues of the times. His Gifford Lectures on *Nature, Man and God* have had a permanent influence on religious thinking. People forget that he was an archbishop and remember that he was the most trusted man in Christendom as he worked to bring the churches together in the World Council of Churches.

Temple did not want to be headmaster of Repton, but he changed his mind. Many years later he described how he made his decision:

I had once to make a choice I found very difficult. . . . I tried to avoid it. . . . I had to make a decision in time to write a letter by a certain post, and having weighed up the question as carefully as I could—and we must always do that—and having come to no conclusion at all, I began at eight o'clock in the evening to say my prayers, and for three hours, without a pause, I tried to concentrate all my desires on knowing clearly what was God's Will for me. I do not know how these three hours went; they did not seem very long; but when eleven o'clock struck I knew perfectly well what I had got to do, and that was to accept; and I have never had a shadow of doubt since that it was right. . . . Each man has to find his own vocation. Every man is able to find that out if, quite sincerely, he will seek to do, not his own will, but God's.[6]

We can learn much from Temple on how to make our decisions. He never failed to use his brains and to consider all the possible problems, but in the end he submitted his decision to the will of God.

He saw God at work in the world and in the Church. In describing the world-wide Christian fellowship, when he was enthroned as Archbishop of Canterbury, he spoke of the World Council of Churches:

As though in preparation for such a time as this, God has been building up a Christian fellowship which now extends into every nation, and binds citizens of them all together in true unity and mutual love. . . . Almost incidentally this great world-fellowship has arisen; it is the great new fact of our era; it makes itself apparent from time to time in World Conferences such as in the last twenty years have been held at Stockholm, Lausanne, Jerusalem, Oxford, Madras, Amsterdam.[7]

During the Edinburgh Conference in 1937, a young American clergyman remembers the charming hospitality of the Archbishop and Mrs. Temple, "taking their place in the common life of Cowan House amid the hundred odd members of the Conference who have their temporary residence in that university hostel. It is a motley assembly. Every main element of the Conference is represented. Quietly, unostentatiously, with a true grace and simplicity, these two move among their fellows, never dining in the same place, taking care without seeming to do so that none are slighted or left to themselves, seeking to learn of the things dear to other Christians. In one sense, it was a little thing. The Archbishop and Mrs. Temple would say so. Probably they thought nothing in particular of their conduct and demeanor during those sixteen days. But to one American at least, whose eyes were upon them, theirs was an inspiring witness."[8]

His last book was called *The Church Looks Forward*. It closes with these words:

The throne of the united world is not a Chair of State; its emblems are not sceptre, orb, and sword; it is a Cross, and the crown is made with thorns. It is as worshippers at the Cross of Christ that we set ourselves to win for the world true peace.[9]

## MARIAN ANDERSON

If you have heard Marian Anderson sing in a concert, on the radio, or on records, you have felt the serenity of her personality. She was the first of her race to sing with the Metropolitan Opera.

Her childhood was uneventful, partially because at an early age she had become a calm and mature person. Beginning as a choir singer, her natural ability was immediately apparent, and her congregation at the Union Baptist Church in Philadelphia helped her start her training. After some study in Germany, she became the rage on the Continent and in South America. Just before her ship arrived home, she broke her ankle, and she sang her first concert at Town Hall on one leg!

She has met prejudice. The Daughters of the American Revolution refused to let her sing in Constitution Hall in Washington, D.C., but as a result she sang before 75,000 people on an Easter morning before the Lincoln Memorial. When prejudice raises its ugly head, she says, "Religion, the treasure of religion helps one, I think, to face the difficulties one sometimes meets." She says, without embarrassment, "I do a good deal of praying." When asked about her achievements, she replies, "Grace must come before greatness."

The anxieties of the Negro have more justification than those of the white, because the Negro has more genuine grievances and difficulties. Great strides are being made in industry, sport, and education to overcome the injustice of many customs, but it is a gradual process. One thing the Negro has learned is the healing power of religion.

Arnold Toynbee writes that

the Negro appears to be answering our tremendous challenge with a religious response which may prove in the event, when it can be seen in retrospect, to bear comparison with the ancient Oriental's response to the challenge from his Russian masters. . . . The Negro has adapted himself to his new social environment by rediscovering in Christianity certain original meanings and values which Western Christendom has long ignored. . . . They may be capable of kindling the cold grey ashes of Christianity which have been transmitted to them until, in their hearts, the divine fire glows again.[10]

Does Miss Anderson, living on her beautiful farm in Danbury, have access to the secret of overcoming anxiety because of her race? Or has she a deeper insight than most of us into our common inheritance from Jesus Christ? If the answer is the latter, must we not share in the traditions of the Negro spiritual and in the ecstasy of faith that results from the sure and certain hope of salvation unto eternal life?

## OUR RESPONSIBILITY

Jesus told a story of three men. A man entrusted his property to them. "To one he gave five talents, to another two, to another one, to each according to his ability. Then he went away." (Matthew 25:15, RSV) A talent was a measure of weight, and in silver or gold was worth about $1,000. The men with $5,000 and $2,000 invested their money and made more, but the man with $1,000 buried it for safe keeping. When the master returned, he praised the two investors and gave them additional responsibility, but the one who buried his money was cast out.

This third man said, "I was afraid." He had no faith in life or in God. He was idle and wicked, a good-for-nothing.

The word "talent" has come into modern use from this story. If you invest what you have, either money or ability, it increases in value. If you fail to do so, you will lose even that which you have. You are not condemned for having one talent or praised for having five talents. You are judged on how you use the gifts God has given you.

No one expects you to be a Barnabas, an Alexander Cummins, a Johann Sebastian Bach, a William Temple, or a Marian Anderson. When Jesus spoke of great works, he mentioned giving a cup of water to the thirsty. A little act to help "the least of these, my brethren," is significant. When Jesus pointed to someone qualified for the kingdom of God, he pointed to a little child and not to a budding genius.

*Great Christians are made.* They are made great by the grace of God when they dedicate whatever they have to God's service. When you watch a symphony orchestra, you see a man sitting and doing nothing, but all at once he becomes alert and brings his instrument to his lips. For just one note, the sound of a piccolo is essential to the full impact of the music.

We need prophets of the stature of a Cummins or a Temple, but unless their vision is caught by the people who hear them, nothing is likely to happen. We need Bach's music, but we need also the insignificant organist that he was considered to be by his contemporaries. We need Marian Anderson's voice, but we need many lesser voices in choirs and concerts and around the camp fire.

Until one-talent people use their ability in God's service, dedicated five-talent people are going to be frustrated in their attempts to make the world a better place in which to live. What's wrong with the world is people, as Will Rogers said; but what's right with the world is people, too. Great Christians are made when they are exposed to the power of God. Saints are everyday people who love the Lord. We have a great heritage in the saints of the past, who live today in stained glass windows and story books, but they did not know they were destined for a "hall of fame."

> They lived not only in ages past,
> There are hundreds of thousands still,
> The world is bright with the joyous saints
> Who love to do Jesus' will.

This hymn makes saintliness less dramatic than the holiness of the headliners of the past, but it makes the saints seem much more alive. "The communion of saints" is "the community of all faithful people." What the world needs is more ordinary, one-talent saints. The little anxieties of people outside the headlines are just as serious as the anxieties of the headliners, and their anxieties are overcome in the same manner. God, who gives us our talents, also gives us the grace to achieve the maturity that helps us not to be anxious. Within our limitations and aptitudes, we, too, may become loyal servants of God. Of such saints, we sing,

> You can meet them in schools, or in lanes, or at sea,
> In Church, or in trains, or in shops, or at tea,
> For the saints of God are just folk like me,
> And I mean to be one, too.[11]

# CHAPTER NINE

# The Lark Is in the Sky

There are many ways God uses to reach men. In the previous chapter, we saw how five people responded. Now we turn to look at four more people whose responses have found other categories. Studdert-Kennedy was a chaplain and a poet whose legacy comes down to us in his writings. John Oxenham was a business man who made writing an avocation. Madeleine Barot wanted to be an archeologist and became a leader of the French underground. Frank Sibilia was a barber and learned to serve God through "vocational giving." They found that through love and work, the lark in the sky sings to the glory of God.

## *STUDDERT-KENNEDY*

Geoffrey A. Studdert-Kennedy was a chaplain in World War I. Out of the anguish of this experience, he came to a knowledge of the suffering of God. God, he said, is like a father who allows his children to make mistakes, for there is no other way for them to learn, and yet God suffers by sharing our suffering.

> So the Father God goes sorrowing still
> For 'Is world what 'as gone to sea,

97

But 'E runs up a light on Calvary's 'eight
That beckons to you and me.
The beacon light of the sorrow of God
'As been shinin' down the years,
A-flashin' its light through the darkest night
O' our 'uman blood and tears.[1]

Studdert-Kennedy saw the sorrow of God against the background of man's disobedience, and at the same time he saw the glory of man's stature as a child of God. He saw life from the perspective of the Master, who was Lord of life on the cross and who also was Lord of life among the lilies of the field. He saw Jesus in the carpenter shop and on the highways as our eternal contemporary, and he saw him living today in the sacraments of the Church. He could see the presence of the living Christ in a little child being baptized, and he knew that Christ was with the soldiers in the trenches.

Because he knew the glory of work and the beauty of the world, he wrote a hymn that is a rhapsody to the glory of God:

Awake, awake to love and work!
The lark is in the sky,
The fields are wet with diamond dew,
The worlds awake to cry
Their blessings on the Lord of Life
As he goes meekly by.[2]

This is a far cry from the complaint, "Oh, how I hate to get up in the morning." In him we see the zest of living life abundantly. Here is the echo of Jesus' words:

Consider the lilies of the field, how they grow; they toil not, neither do they spin: And yet I say unto you, That even Solomon in all his glory was not arrayed like one of these. . . . Therefore do not be anxious, saying, 'What shall we eat?' or 'What shall we drink?' or 'What shall we wear?' . . . But seek first his kingdom and his righteousness, and all these things shall be yours as well. (Matthew 6:28-29, KJ; 6:31,33, RSV)

This does not mean that we do not plan our work. Studdert-Kennedy was a realist about work. He knew that it could be hard and dangerous, routine and monotonous, joyful and creative. He did not have a "whistle while you work" attitude. He could pray:

> Because this is my work, O Lord,
> It must be thine;
> Because it is a human task
> It is divine.[3]

This strong sense of vocation was applied by Studdert-Kennedy to shop and store, factory and office, home and school. He saw work as significant partly because he could imagine Jesus in the carpenter's shop, working with wood to create the structures of people's homes. One of his poems speaks of factory workers, and miners, and concludes:

> When on the sweat of labour and its sorrow,
> Toiling in twilight, flickering and dim,
> Flames out the sunshine of the great tomorrow,
> When all the world looks up—because of Him.

> Then will He come—with meekness for His glory,
> God in a workman's jacket as before,
> Living again the Eternal Gospel Story,
> Sweeping the shavings from His workshop floor.[4]

Christian faith sees "the lark in the sky" during the darkest nights of the soul. Christians neither escape from evil nor resign themselves to it, but they seek to overcome evil with good. Studdert-Kennedy's faith was not destroyed during those terrible years in France in World War I. He saw more clearly that suffering is the price that we have to pay for our freedom and for

99

the opportunity to serve God, and he saw that God's suffering love is great enough for men to know they are accepted even in the midst of such horror. He saw men giving up their lives, and he knew that God was with them.

We can transcend our fears and worries and anxieties by joining the great company of faithful people whose voice is hope, whose eyes are faith, and whose heart is love.

> Come, let thy voice be one with theirs,
> Shout with their shout of praise;
> See how the giant sun soars up,
> Great Lord of years and days!
> So let the love of Jesus come
> And set thy soul ablaze. . . .

Souls on fire burn up their troubles. Souls, indwelt by the flame of the Spirit of God, consume the impurities of their own natures. Souls, caught up in the blaze of the consuming love of God, are raised to the light that makes all things shine in the reflection of his glory!

Our human spirits by themselves are like flickering candles, and the winds of misfortune may snuff them out. In our own selves, we do not have an eternal flame fed by the unending love of God. The source of the soul's flame is God, and he feeds the human soul when we turn in the right direction.

> So let the love of Jesus come,
> And set thy soul ablaze,
> To give and give, and give again
> What God hath given thee;
> To spend thyself nor count the cost,
> To serve right gloriously
> The God who gave all worlds that are,
> And all that are to be.[5]

The richest Christian lives are those dedicated to the service of others and of God. This does not mean that everyone must be a Studdert-Kennedy, a David Livingstone, or an Albert Schweitzer, but it does mean this: *whatever our vocations, whatever our opportunities, whatever our circumstances, whatever our aptitudes, those who give of themselves receive the blessings of God.*

This was true of Studdert-Kennedy, who burned himself out in his work. It is true of many parents, whose souls are miraculously strengthened and refreshed as they serve and guide their children. But the motivation must be right! We know parents who lavish their love on their children in order to satisfy the parents' need for power, and this "smother" love destroys the relationship of parent and children.

When trouble brews in any community, people appear from nowhere to meet the needs of those in difficulty. They provide a little help here and there, buckle down to the problem at hand, organize neighbors when necessary, and clear the situation. It is true that people who "give and give, and give again" have their own troubles, but because their thoughts are centered outside themselves their troubles are never magnified by anxieties and worries. They see, with Ralph Waldo Emerson,

> . . . in the mud and scum of things,
> There alway, alway something sings.[6]

Studdert-Kennedy saw men short-circuiting the power of God by refusing to be channels of grace. This is illustrated by a conversation between William Temple and him on the subject of God's forgiveness. Forgiveness, he thought, is something that permeates the Christian fellowship.

The priest, as the organ and mouthpiece of such a society, could give assurance to the penitent that his sin did not exclude him from this movement of divine forgiveness in the Christian fellowship, but that in virtue of his penitence he was free of it. *But where the actual members were selfish, censorious, unsympathetic—there the priest could only declare the divine goodwill to the sinner; he could not in the same way actually convey it, because the selfishness of the society for which he acted blocked its effective flow.*[7]

Do you see how you fit into God's divine plan? A man in his loneliness may be damned, and his spiritual isolation from God and his fellows is his damnation. As members of God's beloved community, we are the means of creating the fellowship whereby our companions on the way may be saved. Our own anxieties are overcome not by our own efforts, but as we forget them in helping others to overcome their anxieties. As we seek to bring them into the fellowship of love, we find that the love that draws them in banishes our anxieties and fears. Therefore, we are restored to fellowship with God as we become true fellows within the congregation.

## JOHN OXENHAM

Most of us know John Oxenham as a poet who wrote "In Christ there is no East or West." He began his career as an editor and advertising man and was successful in Fleet Street. When he began to write, he kept his identity a secret. His real name was William A. Dunkerley, and he led a double life as a business man and a novelist. John Oxenham, as a writer, was never seen by anyone, and he could be reached only through correspondence. His daughter, as she tells his story, refers to him as "J.O."

J.O. believed in work and stuck to his jobs in much the same way as Studdert-Kennedy, and he could express how important work is:

Upon thy bended knees, thank God for work!
In workless days all ills and evils lurk;
For work to do, and strength to do the work,
We thank thee, Lord.[8]

One of his hymns expresses the same insight:

His service is life's highest joy.
It yields fair fruit a hundred fold:
Be this our prayer—'Not fame, nor gold,
But—thine employ.'[9]

His faith was evident in many of his writings, especially
in the later novels, such as *The Hidden Years*. This book
aroused much controversy because it dealt chiefly with the years
of Jesus' life about which we know so little. J.O. introduced
two new characters into the Gospel story, a mongrel dog named
Tobias and a young maiden named Zerah who loved Jesus.
When the reader sees Zerah appear, it seems inevitable that she
should be there, for her beauty and character are worthy of one
who loves the young Nazarene. It is a gripping story, and nothing is quite as overwhelming as seeing the crucifixion through
Zerah's eyes.

J.O. had an interesting reason for remaining anonymous.
He wrote that he had observed "the frantic and illegitimate
attempts of some [men] to build up reputations from the outside, while lacking the inward fire," and that "that had set me
to trying whether an absolutely unknown man could get a
footing without any adventitious aids whatever."[10] He proved
that it could be done.

According to J.O., what makes a writer are:

Patient Endurance,
Dogged Determination,
And a Hopefulness which refuses to die, no matter how it is
maltreated.

These are pounded into him by force of circumstances. And they are good for a man, though it may take him some time to learn that particular lesson.[11]

His novels, pageants, plays, and poems sold well in the years when J.O. was in his prime, and *Bees in Amber* especially is still a popular item. One critic suggested that one reason for his success is "that his poems are prayers and not preachings," and that he never loses sight of real people.

J.O.'s faith provided serenity and confidence for himself and for those who read his works. He had prophetic vision and insight. He believed that we need "to think large and to think beautiful." He loved his fellows and God, and throughout his writings is the "the high eternal gain" of immortality. His greatest hymn concludes:

> Join hands, then, brothers of the faith,
> Whate'er your race may be!
> Who serves my Father as a son
> Is surely kin to me.
>
> In Christ now meet both East and West,
> In him meet South and North,
> All Christly souls are one in him,
> Throughout the whole wide earth.[12]

## MADELEINE BAROT

During World War II, many of us found that external circumstances changed our plans. Many careers of young men were postponed or altered because of war conditions. New opportunities to serve one's fellows, one's country and one's God appeared, and the more heroic of us rose to the challenges before us.

One of these was Madeleine Barot, a French girl who was an excellent student of archeology, studying on the Prize of

Rome fellowship. She was interned for a while, but finally returned to Paris at the same time that the German army arrived. The ruthless imprisonment of the political enemies of the Nazis, including Jews and liberals among many others, led Madeleine Barot in September of 1939 to found the Comité Inter-Mouvements Auprès Des Évacués, known to us as CIMADE. The chief problem was to get into the concentration camps with spiritual help and material aid. This was both difficult and dangerous.

Mademoiselle Barot managed to get into several camps and observe how appalling the conditions were. She felt that only by having representatives of her movement in a camp could her work be accomplished. Two girls submitted to voluntary arrest and remained in one camp for four years, establishing contact with the inmates and acting as intermediaries to provide help from the outside. The French police helped her as she set up teams in other camps.

One of the most serious problems to be faced was the removal of Jews, including Protestants of Jewish descent, to Germany in order to put them to death. The CIMADE workers managed to find out the identity of the victims by number just before they were to be transported to Germany and smuggled as many of them as possible out of the camps. The organization became more complex as these problems were faced and solved.

But then came a new problem. The people who were smuggled out of the concentration camps had to be cared for. They might be captured by the Germans; France could not absorb them all; and the Spanish border was difficult to cross. An agreement was made with Switzerland to take many of them. Sometimes the refugees were hidden in convents until they could escape to a safe haven.

Since the war, CIMADE has faced the refugee problem. No

longer do CIMADE workers lose their lives or risk the danger of imprisonment when identified. CIMADE is out of the underground and is working among the war victims. Madeleine Barot's organization worked in bombed-out towns, sending in American and British young people to help heal the spiritual wounds of those who had lost their homes because of bombs dropped by American and British planes. Some French were opposed to her movement because it helped everyone, especially Jews and liberals, and it even sent teams into Germany after the war. The Germans were helped by this movement of lay Christians working together to heal the wounds of war, sending impoverished German students to study in France, and establishing centers in German cities.

Madeleine sees CIMADE as a Christian activity, as she works to break down the barriers of nationality and language and to bring Christians to a vision of a world church. "Enlightened faith," she says, "is the motive power that widens horizons."[13]

## FRANK SIBILIA

We easily see the marks of Christian vocation in the ministry of Studdert-Kennedy, the writings of John Oxenham, and the Joan of Arc stature of Madeleine Barot. But it was a barber who developed the concept of "vocational giving" on a level that is relevant immediately to all of us.

If you should go into the barber shop in the "bottom of the Mark" (Mark Hopkins Hotel, San Francisco), you would be met by Frank Gerald Sibilia. As he cut your hair, he would start talking about his church, and if you showed any interest he would tell you his story and probably give you a reprint of a magazine article about him.

Frank Sibilia grew up in Newport, Rhode Island, and his father was a barber. He left school at the end of the eighth grade and made his way to California before he was twenty. In time he became the owner of a barber shop in San Francisco. He was an active member of a little church that met in a store near his home in Berkeley. He wondered how he, as a barber, could serve his church. What he wanted most was to see the congregation have its own lot and its own building. He conceived the idea of cutting the hair of the parishioners in his spare time, and they could place their money in the building fund. So "vocational giving" was born. He fixed up a barber shop in his home, and on Sunday afternoons and after getting home at night, he cut hair and talked of his dream of a new church.

The spirit of his work soon reached across the bay to his shop. He was so enthusiastic about his project that he talked to his customers. Some of them became interested, and after paying him for their haircuts, shaves, shampoos, or other niceties of barbering, they added donations for the building fund. Sibilia had some special envelopes printed and kept track of every donation in a little black book. His minister sent acknowledgments to every donor.

Here were average people, coming to a fashionable barber shop and talking naturally about religion. In 1945, through his work alone, over $1,400 was donated to the building fund. In 1946, a customer sent a check for $1,000 after hearing Sibilia's story. One of his customers was a retired admiral and Sibilia used to go to his room and cut his hair and talk about his church. The admiral would occasionally write out a check. One time, Sibilia discussed with the admiral an idea for buying a new automobile for his minister, and the admiral wrote a substantial check to start the special project. Sibilia regularly went to his bishop's office to cut hair, and always there was a

$5 donation for the fund. Whenever he served a clergyman, he accepted nothing for himself but placed the whole amount in the building fund.

"Vocational giving" caught on first in his own congregation, St. Alban's Protestant Episcopal Church, Albany, California. Other members sought ways in which they could become "vocational givers." As accountants, bankers, salesmen, secretaries, research chemists, and others found ways of cooperating with Sibilia's plan, it was not long before they had a building of their own costing $50,000.

This is an old idea of serving God with one's skill, one's job, and one's hobbies. Many churches have been built when men turned to carpentering and painting in their spare time. Many parishes have been strengthened by the Lord's Acre plan, in which the farmers give the produce of one acre out of ten to the work of the church. Women's groups have served the church with their skills. The possibilities are endless.

Publicity came to "vocational giving" through newspaper stories, articles in magazines, and radio. A TV show had him shave the announcer while he was telling his story. In 1949, at the General Convention in San Francisco, he followed the Presiding Bishop Henry Knox Sherrill as a speaker and was introduced by Harvey Firestone, Jr. Since then, his diocese has sent him to two General Conventions.

When the debt on the $50,000 building was finally paid off, it was estimated that in one way or another Frank Sibilia had raised $30,000 of the total. And now he continues his project for the next building that is needed.

Throughout it all, Sibilia has felt that this outpouring of his spirit has kept him balanced and sane and happy. It has deepened his sense of vocation, because he knows that as a barber he is serving his Lord. He likes the publicity, and he is in constant demand as a speaker at church groups. He sums up his message as follows:

Though we give of our substance, we can also give of our vocation in direct service to God. Vocational giving is simply the giving of our extra labor and extra income derived from our work and in relationship to the congregation of the church. It does not matter what job one has! There is work to be done, and consecrated imagination can discover it! The strange thing is that as one gives of his vocation for the strengthening of the church, his own business prospers. Try it in your own life and see.

## VOCATION

As we have looked at these people in the last two chapters, we discover that they had a sense of vocation, that is, they were called by God to their tasks. The sense of vocation arises *after* one has made an act of commitment. The letter to the Ephesians says that *because* you are saved by God's acceptance of you, *therefore* you are to be worthy of your calling (Ephesians 4:1). "Grace was given to each of us according to the measure of Christ's gift" (Ephesians 4:7, RSV), and your calling is different from mine.

When we know that God is at work in the world and in us, and when we trust him and his purpose for us, we have faith. Our faith is our decision to trust in him and to accept the grace he offers us. Daniel Day Williams writes that we need to understand that *"the living God whose nature and purpose is love calls us to respond in our freedom to the tasks which are set for us by the fact that He is at work in our human history both as Creator and as Redeemer."* [14]

When we come to the realization that God has come into history especially in Jesus Christ to restore our relationships with him, our attitudes and relationships toward others are transformed. Our new decisions are made in the light of this transformed relationship with God and with our fellows. Because our anxieties have been overcome through faith, we are free to make decisions as to how we are called to serve him.

There is nothing magical about the sense of vocation. We have to figure it out. Frank Sibilia, as a barber, asked himself how he could turn a job into a vocation, and he found the answer. A housewife may ask herself how she can turn the drudgery of housework into a vocation, and she may seek the answer in labor saving devices and still think of it as drudgery; or she may see that her vocation as wife and mother makes her work a glorious task with or without gadgets. Alexander Miller suggests that we can test a doctrine of vocation on a New York taxi driver, for he suspects that if the Protestant doctrines of forgiveness and justification by faith are used, and if the tests of highly developed skills and social usefulness are applied, the cab driver would pass the test.[15]

A letter from the church in Jerusalem to Barnabas and Paul gave them some advice on how to get along among the heathen, and they prefaced this advice with these words: "For it seemed good to the Holy Ghost and to us" (Acts 15:28, KJ). "For the Holy Spirit and we have decided" (G) what your burden should be. The job we are called to do may be monotonous, exhausting, and unchallenging. It may be creative, refreshing, and a genuine test of our abilities. But even the routine task may be transformed because of our attitude toward it.

The test of our work is that it be socially useful and worthwhile, that it make use of what abilities we have, and that it provide a chance for us to grow. Not all jobs fit this ideal, but when we find one that does we had better stick to it. Then the test turns from the worthwhile task to ourselves, for we need to face our vocation with integrity, creativity, imagination, and love. At this point, the significance of our work and the calibre of our attitude will unite in the end result of social contributions of significant proportions.[16]

Two doctors were in the same sanitarium as patients. One was a medical doctor with arthritis; the other was a psychiatrist with tuberculosis. Both had given up all hope, for they had diagnosed themselves and were resigned to their fate. They met and began comparing notes, and each became interested in the other. They forgot themselves as they concentrated on the welfare of the other, and soon the zest for life returned. Each man prescribed for the other, and while the prescriptions helped considerably, the mental attitude of each underwent a profound change. With the proper treatment and the forgetting of self, each began to show improvement. The psychiatrist's tuberculosis was healed and he returned to his practice. The doctor with arthritis was too crippled to return to his practice, but his illness was arrested and he adjusted himself to his limited activities. These men, who had been turned inward and would have died, were turned outward by the need of the other, and they learned to live.

Souls set on fire with the love of Jesus Christ burn up their troubles in this same way. When we spend ourselves and do not count the cost, we find that we are truly alive. The lark can be in the sky for everyone, as it was for Studdert-Kennedy and John Oxenham, who learned that by giving themselves with abandon they found the "abundant life" that Jesus promised to his disciples. Madeleine Barot knows this as she struggles among the refugees of Europe for a new chance to live a decent life. Frank Sibilia has experienced the same glory of giving from the perspective of his barber shop. It is simply a matter of learning

> *To give and give, and give again,*
> *What God hath given thee.*

# CHAPTER TEN

# A Vigorous and Vital Faith

When we read the New Testament, we often find a challenge of goals to be achieved and a vision of the world to be. When we turn to the hymns of the church, we sing, "Onward, Christian soldiers," who "fight the good fight" and they "stretch every nerve and press with vigor on." We hear the "Master say, 'Go, work today!'" We come to the conclusion that Christianity is a vigorous and vital faith.

St. Paul has been called "the athletic coach" of our faith. If we had learned when we were young that we should be athletes of religion, we would grasp more easily the idea that religious faith expresses itself in what William James called "toughmindedness." His faith was "healthy-minded." Listen to St. Paul:

Do you remember how, on a racing track, every competitor runs, but only one wins the prize? Well, you ought to run with your minds fixed on winning the prize! Every competitor in athletic events goes into serious training. Athletes will take tremendous pains—for a fading crown of leaves. But our contest is for an eternal crown that will never fade.

I run the race then with determination. I am no shadowboxer. I really fight! I am my body's sternest master, for fear that when I have preached to others, I should myself be disqualified. (I Corinthians 9:24-27, P)

It is important to remember that this passage was written by St. Paul, who was no mean athlete of Christianity in his own right. His vigorous ministry in the face of constant risk led to the establishment of Christian churches throughout the Greek and Roman world. His risks involved both physical and spiritual hardships. In a moment of claiming his right as a preacher, he listed his recommendations.

"This is a silly game," he wrote,

But look at this list:
I have worked harder than any of them.
I have served more prison sentences.
I have been beaten times without number.
I have faced death again and again.
I have been beaten the regulation thirty-nine stripes by the Jews five times.
I have been beaten with rods three times.
I have been stoned once.
I have been shipwrecked three times.
I have been twenty-four hours in the open sea.
In my travels I have been in constant danger from rivers and floods, from bandits, from my own countrymen, and from pagans. I have faced danger in city streets, danger in the desert, danger on the high seas, danger among false Christians. I have known exhaustion, pain, long vigils, hunger and thirst, doing without meals, cold and lack of clothing. . . .
Oh, if I am going to boast, let me boast of all the things I was not clever enough to dodge! The God and Father of our Lord Jesus Christ knows that I speak the truth.
In Damascus, the town governor, acting on King Aretus' order, had men out to arrest me. I escaped by climbing through a window and being let down the wall in a basket. That's the sort of dignified exit I can boast about. (II Corinthians 11:23b-27,30-33, P)

The vigorous and vital Paul had a right to talk about religion. There is no doubt about his qualifications. He was a good coach because he had played the game up to the hilt. When he talked about self-restraint and serious training, with his body under subjection, he knew what he was talking about. He had been at the training table with his Lord, and so he ran toward his goal without swerving and with determination. None of his well aimed blows swished through the air, and you will find no wild haymakers among his pointed remarks. He was never disqualified, because he practiced what he preached, and when he was foolish enough to brag, he could list achievements great enough to put all his rivals to shame.

When one has this kind of faith, there is no room for anxiety. A vigorous and vital faith is a growing faith. Paul's emphasis was on "so run, that you *may* obtain" (KJ). "You ought to run with your minds fixed on winning the prize!" (P) It is not like an earthly track meet at which there is only one winner. Salvation is for all, provided one keeps the faith. But none of us has salvation, and we are merely runners on the straight and narrow way that leads to the kingdom of God.

Paul began with the reminder that an athlete takes seriously his training program. He is temperate and keeps his appetites under control. He abstains from whatever will spoil his prowess and skill. He is a stern master of his body, because he knows that a long distance runner needs endurance.

The Christian takes this advice seriously. Paul was not talking about spiritual training alone. His own trials and tribulations make it evident that physical condition is as important as spiritual condition. He really meant that the Christian should refrain from acts that spoil his physical well being, being temperate about drinking and getting sufficient exercise and rest.

The ascetics of the Church, especially those in the monasteries, maintained this careful subjection of the body, although they often overdid the regimentation and spoiled their health.

We see such careful discipline in such great Christians as Ignatius Loyola, who followed a strict military regime and inflicted it on his followers. We see it in the lives of missionaries who accept the most primitive conditions in order that the Gospel may be lived with the people. But the well conditioned athlete is not worth much if he does not participate in the race of life, just as the man who prays and takes no steps to correct his faults finds that his prayers are irrelevant. The churchgoer in the mainstream of Christian living is more to Paul's liking.

## POLYCARP

A Christian is like a good athlete in that he knows where he is going and why. He moves with determination and has no doubt about his goal. His allegiance is clear and beyond doubt. One of the great examples of this was Polycarp, the venerable bishop of Smyrna, who was put to death on February 22, 156 A.D. He had been bishop for forty years and was eighty-six years old. His own people loved and admired him, but he was in trouble with the police for refusing to accept Caesar as a god.

Polycarp expected to be burned because he had had a dream that his pillow was on fire. The police offered him his freedom if he would only admit that Caesar could be worshiped. The chief of police said,

"Why, what harm is there in saying, "Caesar is Lord," and burning incense, and so on, and saving yourself."

At first he made no answer, but when they persisted, he said, "I am not going to do what you advise me."

When they failed to persuade him, they spoke threateningly to him, and put him out of the carriage so hastily that as he got out of it he hurt his shin. Without turning around, he went eagerly on without noticing it, and was taken to the arena, when the uproar in the arena was so great that nobody could be heard.

As Polycarp entered the arena, there came to him a voice from heaven,

"Be strong, Polycarp, and act like a man."

Nobody saw the one who spoke, but those of our people who were there heard the voice. When at length he was brought forward there was a great uproar when they heard that Polycarp had been taken. . . . When the governor insisted, saying,

"Take the oath, and I will let you go; revile Christ," Polycarp said,

"For eighty-six years I have been his slave, and he has done me no wrong; how can I blaspheme my king who has saved me?"

When he still insisted, and said,

"Swear by the fortune of Caesar," he answered,

"If you imagine that I will swear by the fortune of Caesar, as you say, and pretend not to know who I am, let me tell you plainly, I am a Christian. And if you want to learn the doctrine of Christianity, set the day and hear me."

The governor told him to convince the people, then threatened him with wild animals, and finally with fire. Polycarp said,

"You threaten me with the fire that burns for an hour and in a little while goes out, for you do not know about the fire of the coming judgment and everlasting punishment, which is reserved for the wicked. But why do you wait? Bring on whatever you please."

Saying this and much more, he was filled with courage and joy, and his face was filled with graciousness, so that not only did he not collapse at what was said to him, but on the contrary the governor was amazed and sent his own herald to the middle of the arena to announce three times,

"Polycarp has acknowledged that he is a Christian."

That was enough, and soon the firewood was collected by the mob, and Polycarp was burned.[1]

Unless a man is sure of his goal, as Paul wrote, he may be disqualified. To be rejected as worthless after one has confessed his faith in Christ is to be a castaway. Polycarp refused to be thus disqualified after his long and faithful service to Christ. He was vigorous and vital until the end.

## DIETRICH BONHOEFFER

Martyrdom in the twentieth century does not occur very often, and when it does it lacks the publicity of the arena. But the secret police and the character assassins are equally effective. Dietrich Bonhoeffer, who was one of the Christian plotters against the life of Adolf Hitler, who maintained an underground seminary to train men for the ministry during World War II, and who spent much time in prison, was one of the modern martyrs. He sneaked out of his country, at great personal risk, to keep alive the relations of the German church with the World Council of Churches and met with the Bishop of Chichester in Stockholm. He was finally put to death by Storm Troopers without trial.

Bonhoeffer wrote letters and articles, many of which are now appearing as books in English translation. He placed his emphasis on obedience to Jesus Christ, who had paid the price of his salvation by dying for him. There was no room in Bonhoeffer's faith for drawing room discussions or for worship without action. He felt that many churches had cheapened religion until it had no connection with the dynamic faith of the early disciples. One of his earliest books was entitled *The Cost of Discipleship*. "Cheap grace," he wrote, "is the deadly enemy of our Church. We are fighting today for costly grace. . . . Cheap grace means grace sold on the market like a cheapjack's wares. The sacraments, the forgiveness of sin, and the consolations of religion are thrown away at cut prices. . . . Cheap grace means grace as a doctrine, a principle, a system. . . .

Cheap grace means justification of sin without justification of the sinner. Cheap grace is the preaching of forgiveness without requiring repentance, baptism without Church discipline, Communion without confession, absolution without contrition. Cheap grace is grace without discipleship, grace without the Cross, grace without Jesus Christ, living and incarnate."

He contrasted with this the kind of grace he found in the Holy Scriptures and in the biographies of those with a vigorous and vital faith. "Costly grace," he wrote, "is the treasure hidden in the field; for the sake of it a man will gladly go and sell all that he has. . . . Costly grace is the gospel which must be *sought* again and again, the gift which must be *asked* for, the door at which a man must *knock*. . . . Such grace is costly because it costs a man his life, and it is grace because it gives a man the only true life." [2]

Many faithful disciples have shared Bonhoeffer's view of the cost of discipleship. We saw it when Bishop Eivind Berggrav was the center of a resistance movement in Norway during World War II. Otto Dibelius, bishop of Berlin, showed the same kind of courage when the Communists occupied his diocese.

### COURAGE AND SECULARISM

When the opposition to Christianity is clear-cut, it is not difficult to point to the Paul or Polycarp, the Bonhoeffer or Berggrav, who stand against the darkness of greed, power, and sin. When the opposition is more subtle and oblique, it is harder to give evidence of a vigorous and vital faith. Too many people are like shadowboxers who fight by beating the air when they should "stretch every nerve and press with vigor on." When a man's faith is the issue, he will fight with all his might. Under such pressures, a man either will break down or he will respond with a faith that gives meaning to all that he thinks and does. He has no time to become anxious, even though he may be afraid, because his personality is centered in his loyalty to Jesus Christ. He develops maturity, poise, and judgment in the face of a crisis. Nothing that life may do to him can sway him from his loyalty. He has discovered the truth of Jesus' saying: "I tell you, my friends, do not fear those who kill the body, and after that have no more that they can do" (Luke 4:12, RSV).

Our fear of the opinions of our friends and families, our reluctance to face ridicule, our unwillingness to be scoffed at, and our desire to avoid unpopularity often make us hesitate to admit that Christ is at the center of our lives. Polycarp's fear of the lions in the arena or of the fire is as nothing in comparison to the fear of being marked as different from the secular type of the modern world. What is our reaction to Polycarp's words when the soldiers were going to nail him down before burning him?

"Leave me as I am," he said, "for he who enables me to endure the fire will also enable me to stay on the pyre without moving, without your fastening me with nails." [3]

When a man lives in the midst of fear and insecurity, he builds in his life a vacuum. Additional activity acts as a whirl-wind on the outside of the vacuum, but it cannot fill it. This void is negative, and only a positive faith can fill it. So Jesus said, "Do not fear those who kill the body but cannot kill the soul; rather fear him who can destroy both soul and body in hell." (Matthew 10:28, RSV)

The Christian knows that no man can do this to another man. The body, yes, but the soul, no. Not even the worst kind of brainwashing can destroy the soul. The record is clear that resistance to brainwashing is strongest among those who have a positive faith.

Here is the answer to all the pressures of modern life. Here is the source of strength that enables a man to stand for what is right in the midst of all kinds of ethical confusion. Here is the light that shines in darkness. The security of the soul that is loved by God is not threatened by anything that happens to the body.

Christian faith gives us two points of reference that transcend our secular culture. The first is the source of power that comes from God's love revealed in Jesus Christ. This is one aspect of what is meant by God's grace. In the forgiving love of God we find acceptance, and because we are restored to a personal relationship with the divine Person we are enabled to serve him with courage. The second is the frame of reference for our ideals. This is another aspect of God's grace. In the revelation of God as found in history, we discover the transcendent ideals to guide our behavior. The teachings of Jesus, as the culmination of ethical monotheism, are our supreme guide here, although the seeming impossibility of achieving his ideals forces us back to the first aspect of grace, the reliance on God for the power to be obedient servants.

Let us, then, "encouraged by the good examples of the saints, persevere in running the race that is set before us,"[4] "looking unto Jesus, the author and finisher of our faith; who for the joy that was set before him endured the cross, despising the shame, and is set down at the right hand of the throne of God" (Hebrews 12:2, KJ).

# CHAPTER ELEVEN

# The Joy of Believing

A wise Chinese Christian once described what Christianity meant to him. "First," he said, "it took away my fear, then it gave me uncontrollable joy, and finally it got me into a peck of trouble."

The author of the letter to the Hebrews put it this way:

But faith forms a solid ground for what is hoped for, a conviction of unseen realities. The men of old gained approval by it. By faith we understand that the worlds were put to order at God's command so that what we now see did not come from visible things. (Hebrews 11:1-3, VK)

He described what faith had done for the heroes of the past and provided a list of men and women who were examples of Old Testament faith. We, too, should consider these witnesses, and run our own race with our eyes "fixed on Jesus, the Source and Goal of our faith. . . . Think constantly of him enduring all that sinful men could say against him, and you will not lose your purpose or your courage." (Hebrews 12:4, P)

## FEAR

The answer to all kinds of fear is faith. The first thing that Christ does for us is to cast out fear. Whenever Jesus came up against mental illness or emotional instability, he not only promised forgiveness of sins but he added, "Thy faith hath made thee whole." The paralytic could not get near to Jesus until his friends made a hole in the roof and let him down in the midst of the crowd. Jesus "when he saw their faith, said, 'Man, your sins are forgiven you'" (Luke 5:20, RSV). A man with social position came to see Jesus about his sick servant and told Jesus that if he just said the word, it would be enough. Jesus' reply was, "I tell you, not even in Israel have I found such faith" (Luke 7:9, RSV).

In the midst of all these cures, the followers of John the Baptist came and asked Jesus who he was, and he replied, "Go and tell John what you have seen and heard: the blind receive their sight, the lame walk, lepers are cleansed, the dead are raised up, the poor have the good news preached to them. And blessed is he who takes no offence at me" (Luke 7:22-23, RSV).

But some of the people did take offence at him. After Jesus had healed a dumb man, "some of them said, 'He casts out demons by Beelzebub, the prince of demons'" (Luke 11:15, RSV). "His relatives heard of it and came over to stop him, for they said that he was out of his mind." (Mark 3:21, G) Even his mother and his brothers heard about it, and they tried to get through the crowds to see him and take him home, but he rejected them and said, "'Who are my mother and my brothers?' . . . . 'Whoever does the will of God is my brother and sister and mother'" (Mark 3:33,35, G).[1]

His defense was simple: "'How can Satan drive Satan out? If a kingdom is disunited, that kingdom cannot last?'" (Mark 3:23b-24, G.) One can cast out demons only "by the finger of God."

Some psychologists have tried to make a case for Jesus' mental unbalance. They have claimed that Jesus had a messianic complex, and they point to the Gospel according to John for the evidence. Professor C. C. McCown provided the key to this problem by saying that

a very large proportion of the arguments used to prove that Jesus was a paranoic or otherwise mentally unstable have been drawn from the Fourth Gospel. . . . The answer given by the great majority of critics . . . is that the discourses at least are not historical.[2]

The historical answer is found in the first three Gospels. The record shows that Jesus was accused of being "deranged" (VK), "out of his mind" (G, M, W), or "mad" (K). He defended himself by showing that an agent of evil could not exorcise evil. He had no illusions about himself and was careful about any claims to messiahship. If he was not a fraud, he was what the Church has believed him to be: the Christ or the "anointed one."

For the Christian believer, the resurrection story has always been the clinching argument. This was the experience that converted the members of Jesus' own family. It was the main point in Paul's address to the Athenians. Jesus' followers were convinced, not only that he was sane, but that he was anointed by God for a special task, which is what "Christ" or "Messiah" means. "In Christ God was reconciling the world to himself." (II Corinthians 5:19)

Christianity, when properly understood, is the surest basis for mental and spiritual health. The overpowering personality of Jesus as the living Christ provides wholesome truth and dynamic power for today, just as the Jesus portrayed in the Gospels provided integrative strength for his disciples.

Let us see how this is done. Mental health depends on the integration of the personality. Integration is a harmony of wholesome attitudes, emotions, and appetites, depending on singleness of purpose and the meaningfulness of one's goal.

There is a dominating sentiment that holds the personality together. The richness of this integration depends on the level of the goal and the richness of the variety within a single purpose. This purpose, furthermore, must be within the limits of our present personalities at its beginning and then catch us at our "growing edge" in order to lead us to higher levels of spiritual growth.

The Christian Gospel has always claimed to do exactly this. The New Testament message calls sinners to repentance, and this is always the starting point. The person who is integrated on a low level, or who is slowly disintegrating due to the misuse of his appetites, or who is distraught or distressed, or who is seeking for a higher way but lacks adequate motivation, finds in the living Christ the dynamic force that will lead him in new directions.

At the beginning, it is a matter of experimental faith, a willingness to make an investment of what is left of the self, a desire to turn from the dissatisfactions of living on a lower level, an admission of sin and guilt, a profound determination to seek what God has to offer. And he comes up against the promise of Biblical religion: "Seek and ye shall find. . . . Ask and it shall be given you."

This leads to the major change that is essential for overcoming anxiety and fear. The Christian faith leads a man away from himself. Because many forms of spiritual and mental illness are due to a concern that turns a man in on himself, this seeking for a personal relationship outside the self is the beginning of the healing process.

The Christian faith centers in God, and God is beyond all human selves. He is the eternal "Thou" with whom we may have a personal and enduring relationship. We are not placing our faith in an *idea* of God, for an idea is never sufficiently dynamic to account for what happens to a true believer. We know the living God, whose chief attribute is love. We achieve the knowledge that is called "saving truth." It is the knowledge that God loves us no matter how unlovely we are, that he will heal our broken relationships with him and with our fellows, and that all we need to do is to accept the fact that he accepts us. We come to believe that "there is no fear in love, but perfect love casts out fear. . . . We love, because he first loved us" (I John 4:18a,19, RSV). Then we are ready for his commandment, "that he who loves God should love his brother also" (I John 4:21, RSV).

## *JOY*

Love not only takes away fear; it works also on the other side. The Chinese Christian said that the second step as a Christian was, "It gave me uncontrollable joy." The Fourth Gospel represents Jesus as saying, "I have come that they might have life, and have it abundantly" (John 10:10, KJ).

The joy of believing is not freedom from pain or tribulation. It is not sheer pleasure. In the Fourth Gospel, joy is seen against the background of the peril and pain of childbirth: "You will be sorrowful, but your sorrow will turn to joy. When a woman is in travail she has sorrow, because her hour has come; but when she is delivered of the child, she no longer remembers the anguish, for joy that a child is born into the world. So you have sorrow now, but I will see you again, and your heart will rejoice, and no one will take your joy from you" (John 16:20-23, RSV).

The Christian faith has always brought "tidings of great joy," even in the midst of tribulation. Jesus said that in the midst of persecution, we could "rejoice in that great day, and leap for joy" (Luke 6:22, RSV). Paul's letter to the Romans has this benediction, "So may God, the fountain of hope, fill you with all joy and peace in your believing, so that you may enjoy overflowing hope by the power of the Holy Spirit" (Romans 15:13, VK).

Jesus was accused of being light-hearted. In contrast to John the Baptist, he and his disciples did not fast, they lived in villages and cities, and they attended parties, dinners, and weddings. We often forget this side of the Gospel picture. Jesus was criticized for being the friend of wine-bibbers and sinners. He loved little children and made an easy friendship with them, and even his own disciples disapproved of this lightness of attitude. After the resurrection, the earliest followers of the Way were characterized by a warm, human fellowship, covering every intimate phase of living.

Joy, gladness, happiness, blessedness—these descriptions are found throughout the literature of Christendom. These attitudes are the experience of countless believers. Not possessions or social security or political power, but simple joy is theirs. It is expressed often in the extreme emotional responses of some of the Pentecostal sects, and it is a genuine experience even when it is magnified by overstimulation. We see this joy in the quiet radiance showing on the faces of some Christian mystics, and in the dynamic peace of countless hordes of the faithful throughout the world. It is expressed in worship, in the prayers and psalms and sermons of the churches.

The Beatitudes express the central element of Christian living. "The second, fourth, and sixth Beatitudes," wrote Burton Scott Easton,

describe the inner character of the righteous: evil distresses them; they know they are sinners but long to become better; and their hearts are fixed on a single purpose. The third, fifth, and seventh Beatitudes describe their outward character: they are gentle, merciful, peacemakers. The first and eighth Beatitudes 'frame' the whole: in any civilization whose ideal is success at any cost, such persons are bound to be despised and maltreated.[3]

But they will be happy anyhow, because they will receive their reward from the loving heavenly Father in terms of spiritual blessings, in their wholeness of personality, and in their power for good. For those with this kind of spiritual health, the kingdom of God is theirs.

We see this clearly as we read the Beatitudes in Easton's translation. He has set them in a form that brings out the poetry of the original language:

> Blessed are they who endure despite oppression,
>   For theirs is the Kingdom of God.
> Blessed are they who mourn at unrighteousness,
>   For they shall be comforted.
> Blessed are the gentle,
>   For they shall inherit the promised land.
> Blessed are they who hunger and thirst after righteousness,
>   For they shall be filled.
> Blessed are the merciful,
>   For they shall obtain mercy.
> Blessed are the pure in heart,
>   For they shall see God.
> Blessed are the peacemakers,
>   For they shall be called 'Sons of God.'
> Blessed are they who are persecuted for righteousness' sake,
>   For theirs is the Kingdom of God.
>                                        (Matthew 5:3-10, E)

It is impossible to attain this Christian blessedness in isolation. You cannot be integrated as a person unless you are oriented in a personal relationship within a community.

This need for community is evident all of our lives. The

family provides it for the very young, and a distorted family life often results in a spoiled, selfish, and sometimes a mentally ill child. We belong to clubs, lodges, secret orders, and other groups because they promise a communal basis for happiness. Such communities, important as they are, often outlive their usefulness. Alumni groups often hang onto their college loyalties and become permanent sophomores in their attitudes about the losses suffered by the football team. This truncated, stifled integration becomes inadequate for meaningful living.

The only community that transcends family, fraternal groups, and the nation is the Church. The Church provides a sense of community that covers the centuries. We are part of the ongoing, continuing stream of God's witnesses. When human ties are broken, God's community remains and points to a fellowship beyond death.

Through the community of God's people we find a center of our loyalty. There is a perspective within the Church that enables us to see our lives within the framework of history. When we have this perspective, laughter and tears are intermingled, farce and tragedy and pure comedy fit into their proper places, and we have a new sense of values, for we see that all of life is meaningful in God's sight.

Membership in the Church gives us a sense of discipleship. No one can be in the Church without facing the challenge of becoming a disciple of Jesus Christ. He, among all men, is worthy of our loyalty and our worship. Our happiness and our integration center in him who never lets us down.

In such a community we find the means of grace by which we are empowered to live as followers of Jesus Christ. "Finally, my brethren, be strong in the Lord, and in the power of his might, that ye may be able to stand against the wiles of the devil." (Ephesians 6:10-11, KJ)

## TROUBLE

Finally, said our Chinese friend, this Christian religion "got me into a peck of trouble." In Luke's form of the Beatitudes, Jesus said, "Blessed are you when men hate you, and when they exclude and revile you, and cast out your name as evil, on account of the Son of man! Rejoice in that day, and leap for joy, for behold, your reward is great in heaven; for so their fathers did to the prophets" (Luke 6:22, RSV).

Those who take their discipleship seriously are likely to get into trouble. Certainly Jesus did. A Scots woman is reported to have objected when some of her friends played golf on Sunday, and she was reminded that Jesus had approved of David's men eating bread from the altar when they were hungry as justification of Jesus' breaking of the Sabbath. Her reply was, "Yes, and I didn't think the better of 'im for it." Jesus annoyed her, as he has annoyed many others with his capacity to get at the root of any question.

When Jesus healed on the Sabbath, people objected; and Jesus said, "I ask you, is it lawful on the sabbath to do good or to do evil, to save life or destroy it?" "But they were filled with fury and discussed with one another what they might do to Jesus." (Luke 6:9,11, RSV) While Jesus normally kept the Sabbath as did any good Jew, he introduced a disturbing freedom by subjecting this law to a higher one. He said,

> The Sabbath was made for man,
> Not man for the Sabbath;
> Therefore man is master of the Sabbath.
> (Mark 9:27-28, E)

If there was anything more sacred to his fellow Jews than the Sabbath, it was the laws about food. All food had to be ceremonially clean. Jesus said,

Hear me, all of you, and understand: there is nothing outside a man which by going into him can defile him; but the things which come out of him can defile him. . . . For from within, out of the heart of man, come evil thoughts, fornication, theft, murder, adultery, coveting, wickedness, deceit, licentiousness, an evil eye, slander, pride, foolishness. All these things come from within, and they defile a man. (Mark 7:14-16,21-23, RSV)

G. K. Chesterton caught the spirit of this when he wrote:

> O God of earth and altar,
>   Bow down and hear our cry,
> Our earthly rulers falter,
>   Our people drift and die; . . .
> From all that error teaches,
>   From lies of tongue and pen,
> From all the easy speeches
>   That comfort cruel men,
> From sale and profanation
>   Of honor, and the sword,
> From sleep and from damnation,
>   Deliver us, good Lord![4]

Christianity has never promised that life would be easy. Jesus promised his disciples that they would be persecuted, but that the reward for their suffering would be joy.

## GOOD NEWS

The Gospel leads us into trouble, because when we seek to be loyal followers of Christ, we are opposed by the forces of greed and pride. We, too, are always in danger of being caught up in the temptations of easy speeches and the sale of our honor, and when we stand up for the hard right against the easy wrong, we gain the rewards of the joy of believing. We cannot seek this joy, for it is a gift of God through the work of the Holy Spirit. We simply trust God and in thankfulness seek to obey him, and the joy is part of our hope of salvation.

# PART IV

# PRAYER AND WORSHIP

# CHAPTER TWELVE

# Lift Up Your Hearts

The chief means whereby the individual comes into the presence of Almighty God is prayer. Through prayer we come consciously into a personal relationship with the living God, and he hears and answers our prayers in his own way. We are assured that we should

> Seek the LORD while he may be found,
>   call upon him while he is near;
> let the wicked forsake his way,
>   and the unrighteous man his thoughts;
> let him return to the LORD, that he may have mercy on him,
>   and to our God, for he will abundantly pardon.
>                               (Isaiah 55:6-7, RSV)

This is all very well, but we come immediately to the problem of what prayer can and cannot do. We are impressed by the claims made by some of the manner in which prayer supports the desire for successful lives. It is used for guidance in business deals, to make friends and influence people, and as a secret weapon in times of danger. Some people feel very strongly that it works in just this way, while others who have attempted to use prayer as a tool have faced failure.

133

## UNANSWERED PRAYER

If we look first at the problem of unanswered prayer, it will lead us to a profounder understanding of what prayer is. Some have prayed that a child's life might be spared, and in God's Providence the child has died. Others have asked for health, wealth, security, and stability, and they have received illness, poverty, precariousness, and instability. Others have set their hearts on solving particular problems, such as the sex of an unborn babe, a promotion or raise in salary, or good weather for a picnic.

A chaplain faced this problem acutely during World War II. He was concerned about the men who had prayed but did not come back. "We had prayed together before the altar, this young pilot and his chaplain. Then he had climbed into his ship and flown away toward the desert with God's blessing and peace in his heart. The plane crashed and the pilot was killed. Only those who believe certain things as he did could see the part that was not sad. He was in God's grace. He was ready to meet death, and that is not sad but glorious. Not everybody could see it that way, but quite a few did."

"Is there such a thing," asked this chaplain, "as getting the breaks in prayer? . . . What sort of extra-special super-powered prayer is needed to make everything turn out the way we want it? There are always more men who pray to come back than there are men who get back. . . . That's why I wish people would stop writing about soldiers who pray and have their prayers answered by not getting killed."

This realism about prayer may lead to the elimination of prayer from one's life. "That's all very well," says the distraught person. "If God's will is to be done anyhow, I'll stop praying. If prayer doesn't help solve my problem, then I'll stop praying."

The only answer is this: If this is what prayer means to you, then you have never prayed. For this science of begging and getting, with no faith in God's love, is not prayer. It is using God as a means to your own ends. It is asking God to be navigator, juvenile court judge, physician, deflector of bullets, and general scapegoat.

If anyone ever deserved to have his prayer answered, it was Jesus in the garden of Gethsemane. When he prayed for his life, that he might be spared the ignominy of the cross and be permitted to continue his earthly fellowship with his friends, he placed prayer in the proper perspective. He had with him Peter, James, and John, and he told them:

"My heart is in bitter anguish. Stay here and keep watch for me."

Then he walked forward a little way and flung himself on the ground, praying that, if it were possible, he might not have to face the ordeal.

"Dear Father," he said, "all things are possible to You, please— let me not have to drink this cup. Yet it is not what I want but what You want." (Mark 14:34-36, P)

## PRAYER IS POWER

Prayer provides a unique power. Prayer is an attitude toward God that makes possible the fulfillment of God's will in us. It is God's way of using us in his service. If Jesus had never prayed, he could not have become God's agent for the redemption of the world.

The familiar story of Abraham Lincoln's insight into the meaning of prayer cannot be repeated too often. When he was asked to pray that God should be on the side of the Union, he replied, "I am not at all concerned about that, for I know that the Lord is always on the side of the right. But it is my constant anxiety and prayer, that I and this nation may be on the Lord's side."

To the complaint of the chaplain of the men who prayed and who did not come back, there is an answer. Their death is not due to faulty prayers. Archbishop William Temple put it this way: "Shall we pray that God will bring them safely home? Yes, certainly—but not chiefly. We know that they in their best moments do not put safety first. No; our first prayer must be that God will keep them steadfast, loyal to him, to country, to comrades. If that loyalty means death, we would not have them kept from death at the cost of disloyalty."

So whether we pray for safety or victory, for picnic weather or the health of a friend, for success in business or the renewal of love, we know that through prayer God's will is done. In prayer we are with God. His strength, comfort, forgiveness, and revelation are given to us.

Prayer is primarily conversation or dialogue. Otherwise we are just talking to ourselves. Prayer is a means by which something is done because we are related to the divine Person who is the source of our being. This communion with God may be expressed in words, song, or silent thoughts. It is a means of grace.

Reinhold Niebuhr has written a prayer that summarizes in a remarkable way our basic relationship with God:

O God, give me the serenity to accept what cannot be changed—
Give me the courage to change what can be changed—
And the wisdom to distinguish the one from the other.   Amen.[1]

Through prayer we become reconciled to what cannot be overcome. We accept ourselves, with our ugly features or odd stature or lack of aptitude for some tasks. We take necessary suffering without bitterness and face death with courage. We make sacrifices for the good of others. We build our treasures where neither moss nor rust corrupts and where thieves do not break through and steal. With this acceptance of God, of the universe, and of ourselves, we find our anxieties vanishing. Those deep-seated worries do not seem so important when we know that God is with us. We learn to accept the good and evil of each day's experience at their face value, knowing that another day will bring new gifts of grace from the loving Father.

Through prayer we are made strong to overcome obstacles. Prayer opens channels through which we regain mental and physical health. It eliminates our worries and anxieties. It makes us more resolute in seeking what is good and pure and lovely. It aids us in putting aside bitterness and grief and despair. It makes possible forgiveness of others. It helps us to turn to the world with renewed hope and faith. It adds to our strength by stimulating our latent energies. It redirects our thoughts and organizes our purposes. It does all these things and many more, and it does them in a way that would be impossible except for prayer. Above all, through prayer we are in direct, personal communion with the living God. While God is always present, in prayer we are conscious of his presence in a distinctive and unique way.

Through prayer we gain insight to see more clearly what God's will is for us. Thus we receive the gift of careful discrimination between what can be accomplished by God's grace and what is inevitable in the providence of God. We see ourselves as we really are, and thus we locate the hidden potentialities that God has placed in us for the doing of his will. We find new values for living, and we begin to see what matters very much and what matters little. We are capable of rearranging our scale of values and to choose between various courses of action, and thus we come closer to God.

## *THE SCOPE OF PRAYER*

Prayer is the heart of Christian living. It is the secret of spiritual health. It is universal in its scope and deals with the broadest as well as the smallest details of life. We must remember, as Charles Henry Brent wrote, that prayer "is not a scattering of good wishes in the air toward someone we desire to serve. Neither is it the vocal or silent utterance of pious hopes in the direction of God."

The universality of prayer is described in Whittier's words:

> I know not where his islands lift
> Their fronded palms in air;
> I only know I cannot drift
> Beyond his love and care.
>
> O brothers! If my faith is vain,
> If hopes like these betray,
> Pray for me that my feet may gain
> The sure and safer way.
>
> And thou, O Lord! by whom are seen
> Thy creatures as they be,
> Forgive me if too close I lean
> My human heart on thee! [2]

The essence of prayer begins with *adoration*. Prayer turns us away from ourselves as the center of our lives is turned to God. We are familiar with the response of adoration as we observe the wonders of nature. The mountains and the canyons, the purple haze and the glowing sunset, the rushing rivers and the splashing waterfalls carry us out of ourselves.

From this we may come to see that in our adoration of the lilies of the field we may also be adoring the Creator. This is a first step toward our meeting with God as God. We hear about God and then we see his hand in the events around us, and finally we come to know him in a personal relationship. This is something too wonderful for us, and we respond with wonder, awe and reverence before the Holy of holies.

Charles Whiston makes a helpful distinction between the foods of reflection and devotion.[3] A man is talking to himself about God when he says, "Bless the LORD, O my soul; and all that is within me, bless his holy name!" (Psalm 103:1) But his mood is that of adoration when he says, "I will extol thee, my God and King, and bless thy name for ever and ever. Every day will I bless thee, and praise thy name for ever and ever." (Psalm 145:1-2, RSV)

This spirit of adoration is closely related to *thanksgiving*. Because of what God has done for us throughout history as well as in our own lives, we are thankful: "We bless thee for our creation, preservation, and all the blessings of this life; but above all, for thine inestimable love in the redemption of the world by our Lord Jesus Christ," as the popular prayer called *A General Thanksgiving* phrases it.

Because God restores us to fellowship with him and with our fellows by the free gift of grace when we trust him, we are thankful for this reconciliation. It is not because of anything that we have done, but only because we have made the decision to trust in him. We find in this relationship with God a source of power to obey him.

So prayer moves through these steps:

I adore thee, holy God of love,

I thank thee, who through Christ reconciled me to thyself,

I give myself to thee, by the power of the Holy Spirit.

We are born as creatures of God. But God wills that we be more than creatures. He seeks us as children who by choice are members of the divine family. He knows that we cannot be full of the joy and peace of believing until we have placed ourselves freely in his hands. He does not force this, but seeks to persuade us to accept his gift of reconciliation. It is for this reason that he forgives us more than seventy times seven. It is for this cause that Jesus Christ died and rose again.

The power to be self-giving comes when we are reborn as new creatures, when we are transformed by the renewing of our minds, when we are made regenerate. In this way, our prayers need always to be in terms of his will and not ours. We seek to be self-giving because only in this way do we fulfill the meaning of our humanity.

This is the crucial point in prayer. Most of us find it difficult to make a total and unconditional act of surrender. We want some kind of a contract that includes clauses in small print allowing us to follow our own wishes in the matter. We want an escape clause if the going gets too rough. When we remember that James, the brother of our Lord, was killed, that Stephen was stoned to death, that Polycarp was burned, and that modern Christians sometimes face unpopularity, suffering, and martyrdom, we begin looking for an escape hatch.

It takes many of us a long time to include self-giving in our prayers. As children we were used to the "Please God, give me . . ." and "Please God bless . . ." prayers, and we rarely advanced to prayers of adoration, thanksgiving, and self-giving despite the fact that the Lord's Prayer includes these attitudes. Only with the gift of Christian maturity do we take this step.

In the framework of our adoration, our giving thanks, and our full commitment to God, we turn to the needs of others. We practice *intercession*. As we pray for others, let our prayers be turned into action. If we pray for the sick, let us be sure that we translate the prayer into deeds. If we pray for those risking their lives in dangerous pursuits, let us show it in our letters and gifts. God pours comfort, strength, and hope into us, that we in turn may pour it into others. Do you know this prayer of mature faith?

Almighty God, we entrust all who are dear to us to thy never-failing care and love, for this life and the life to come; knowing that thou art doing for them better things than we can desire or pray for; through Jesus Christ our Lord. Amen.

We can pray for good causes, but when we do we should enlist in those causes according to our opportunities. The word, "Amen," means "so be it." It is our enlistment in what is mentioned in the prayer. As we become more discriminating in judging what to pray for, God leads us more deeply into the social and political issues that require the action of a Christian conscience.

When we pray for ourselves, we need to remember that prayer is the beginning of action. When we pray for increased efficiency, we need to do our part. When we ask for spiritual power, we need to fulfill spiritual conditions; when we pray for physical changes, we need to meet physical requirements. Without prayer, we are separated from God and his gifts, but with prayer we are enabled by him to achieve his will for us.

> Pray when the morn is breaking,
>   Pray when the noon is bright,
> Pray with the eve's declining,
>   Pray in the hush of night:
> With mind made clear of tumult,
>   All meaner thoughts away,
> Make thou thy soul transparent,
>   Seek thou with God to pray.[4]

## KEEPING THE ROAD OPEN

Prayer is like a road that needs to be kept open. A little used and poorly constructed road is a hindrance to reaching our destination. We need a familiar road, well-paved and constructed, if we want to reach our goal with confidence. We do not want any broken axles, we do not want to become stuck in the mud or sand, and we do not want any delays, especially in an emergency.

When I feel the need of specific help from God, I want the road to the Almighty to be one that I have travelled frequently and recently. If the road is in bad condition or full of detours, I may not be able to travel it in time. And as far as God is concerned, the condition of the road is my responsibility.

If someone should ask you if you have prayed lately, he is asking if your road to God is a smooth highway ready for quick travel. Your answer may be that it is just two ruts, with all kinds of booby traps along the way and overgrown with weeds; or maybe it is virgin territory and you have never been over it.

When the road is completely uncharted, the danger is even greater. The Donner party attempted about a hundred years ago to cross the Sierra Nevada range on what they thought was a short-cut. Winter set in, and most of them never reached their destination, for they were frozen, or starved, to death. So it is an important question, whether there is a road to God that you keep in good condition.

How do we keep the road open? By travelling over it with some degree of regularity. This does not mean that we will be heard if we use words enough, but it does mean that the attitude of prayer on our part will lead to a sense of communion with God throughout the day. Paul expressed it this way: "Be happy in your faith at all times. Never stop praying. Be thankful, whatever the circumstances may be" (I Thessalonians 5:17, P). Any time will do: when we are stopped by a traffic light, when we are washing or shaving, whenever there is routine that does not require our complete attention.

Edmund Vance Cooke thought of prayer as a means of coming into God's presence. The important thing was not what was said, but that the one who prays has the exercise of travelling the road that leads to God.

> But maybe prayer is a road to rise,
> A mountain path leading toward the skies
> To assist the spirit who truly tries.
> But it isn't a shibboleth, creed, nor code,
> It isn't a pack-horse to carry your load,
> It isn't a wagon, it's only a road.
> And perhaps the reward of the spirit who tries
> Is not the goal, but the exercise! [5]

## PRAYER AND LOVE

Jesus told the story of the man who went to his friend at midnight because he needed three loaves of bread to feed an unexpected guest. He kept on knocking until the friend responded and gave him the bread because he was a nuisance. We, also, are to keep asking, seeking, and knocking. We would not give our sons serpents instead of fish, or scorpions instead of eggs. "If you then, who are evil," concluded Jesus, "know how to give good gifts to your children, how much more will the heavenly Father give the Holy Spirit to those who ask him?" (Luke 11:13, RSV)

This suggests that we should be as importunate in prayer as we are with grudging neighbors, but it also suggests that while grudging neighbors have to be dealt with persistently, God's gift of the Holy Spirit is given to us if we simply ask, seek, and knock. We may need to ask persistently to obtain things from other human beings, but we need only ask to obtain God's blessings.

Yet there is a struggle in prayer. We know that Jesus spent all night in prayer, and his struggle in the Garden of Gethsemane was hardly a recitation of a memorized prayer. The struggle in prayer is the attempt to be self-giving in our relationship with God, and that demands constant effort.[6]

The normal prayer in a family contains a list. It is a "catalog" prayer. Usually it begins with "Please God bless—" and then come all the members of the family, the in-laws and the out-laws, the dog and cat. This is a good prayer, for it is intercession, prayer for others, asking simply for God's blessing upon them. It includes them consciously in God's family, and therefore we treat them differently because we have prayed for them.

If we pray for our enemies in the same spirit, it will break down many barriers to personal relations. A man in an office resented his new boss, who had been promoted from a lower position. When he began to pray that God would bless the new man, his resentment slowly melted away and he was able to become more efficient at his own position. Another person believed he had been slighted several times at parties, so he included in his prayers the people who seemed to snub him. Soon he understood that the exclusions were unintentional and made no difference. Often our prayers are the means of opening our own wills so that we are enabled to forgive those who have hurt us and to ask forgiveness of those whom we have injured. This is what Jesus was talking about when he said that we should make peace with our enemies before we come to the altar. If we cannot resolve the broken relationship under our own power, let us pray for them until the breach is healed.

Our prayers of self-giving place real demands on us. Prayer

changes our attitudes and we gain a better perspective. Jesus made this clear. "If you love those who love you," he asked, "what credit is that to you? Even sinners love those who love them. And if you do good to those who do good to you, what credit is that to you? For even sinners do the same. And if you lend to those from whom you hope to receive, what credit is that to you? Even sinners lend to sinners, to receive as much again. But love your enemies, and do good, and lend, expecting nothing in return; and your reward will be great, and you will be sons of the Most High; for he is kind to the ungrateful and selfish. Be merciful, even as your Father is merciful" (Luke 6:32,36, RSV).

"But I *can't* do that!" is the cry. And so we can't—except by prayer. Constant, sincere, and determined prayer is the *only* source of spiritual power. The standard is high, and Jesus expected his followers to meet it. "Judge not," he said, "and you will not be judged; condemn not, and you will not be condemned; forgive, and you will be forgiven; give, and it will be given to you; good measure, pressed down, shaken together, running over, will be put into your lap. For the measure you give will be the measure you get back" (Luke 6:37-38, RSV).

It is too high a goal! It is impossible. But we can pray about it. If the prayer is sincere, and if it is the soul's desire, and if the road to God is kept open, then it is surprising how close we can come. Prayer as a source of power is already incipient action, and it sets in motion forces in us that are not released by any other method.

There is an uncalculating naïveté about Christian living. We do nothing for the sake of a return, and yet there is always the promise that God will reward us. If we obey *for the sake of the reward,* our false motivation spoils the deed; while if we act without thought of the reward, it is given to us.

The essence of prayer is summarized in a few words. The version of the Lord's Prayer in Luke has everything in it:

Father, hallowed be thy name. Thy kingdom come. Give us each day our daily bread; and forgive us our sins, for we ourselves forgive everyone who is indebted to us; and lead us not into temptation. (Luke 11:2-4, RSV)

That is it: the holy God will give us power to accept his rule over us, and this is his kingdom! In God's kingdom there will be bread enough for all. Our sins will be forgiven because we forgive each other. We will no longer be tempted to sin, or to be anxious, or to be frustrated, for God will give his Holy Spirit to everyone who asks for it.

Jan Struther has summarized much of what we have said in this chapter in her hymn:

Lord of all hopefulness, Lord of all joy,
Whose trust, ever childlike, no cares could destroy,
Be there at our waking, and give us, we pray,
Your bliss in our hearts, Lord, at the break of the day.

Lord of all eagerness, Lord of all faith,
Whose strong hands were skilled at the plane and the lathe,
Be there at our labors, and give us, we pray,
Your strength in our hearts, Lord, at the noon of the day.

Lord of all kindliness, Lord of all grace,
Your hands swift to welcome, your arms to embrace,
Be there at our homing, and give us, we pray,
Your love in our hearts, Lord, at the eve of the day.

Lord of all gentleness, Lord of all calm,
Whose voice is contentment, whose presence is balm,
Be there at our sleeping, and give us, we pray,
Your peace in our hearts, Lord, at the end of the day.[7]

# CHAPTER THIRTEEN

# The Refreshment of Christian Worship

More people are attending church on Sundays than ever before in the history of the nation. A greater percentage of the population than ever before is numbered as members of churches. In this era when so many competitors to church-going may be found—gardening, auto trips, radio, television, good books, fellowship in home and family—there are many people in church every Sunday.

Church-going has become a mark of respectability today. Those who are influenced by what the crowd does have discovered that it is fashionable to be seen in church. In some communities, social status depends on which church one attends. These cultural pressures have no particular connection with religious needs, but at least they make it possible for the church to reach more people.

Often these church connections are casual. An old family custom may dictate that one fufills his responsibility to the church through a token pledge of financial support and an appearance at Christmas and Easter and at such family festivals as baptisms and weddings.

Church-going also stems from habit. Many of us began

attending church as children and never were tempted to stop. But some of us moved to a new location where our customs and habits were thrown into confusion, the effort to make a connection with a new church was too demanding and, therefore, we dropped the habit. Others of us find that the habit of church-going is so strong that no changes in external circumstances have any effect on us.

Certain non-religious impulses are involved in church-going. We need to satisfy our yearning for fellowship, and this need is often satisfied in church. People go to church to make friends. They go to make business contacts. They go for any number of personal reasons. And they go because they are anxious about their decisions, their status, and their need for approval.

If church-going depended only on these needs, the future of the Church would be precarious. Whenever the Church depends on these factors, it is using its capital and is not investing for the future. The heart of the Church's life is its worship, and the future of worship depends on its capacity to meet man's fundamental religious needs.

## VALUES OF PUBLIC WORSHIP

One of America's most acute observers of church life and worship was James Bissett Pratt, who wrote that

worship increases one's insight and strengthens one's belief; it tends to induce certain desirable emotional states, such as comfort in sorrow, confidence in anxiety, joy, peace; it helps to give a new direction to the activity of the will in the moral life. [It satisfies] the need that many feel for the recognition of the divine and for the sense of mystic contact with God.[1]

First, corporate worship strengthens religious faith. The Church is a worshiping community, where the barriers of loneliness are battered down by the power of the Holy Spirit. The poet asks:

> What life have you if you have not life together?
> There is no life that is not in community,
> And no community not lived in praise of God.[2]

When we are reinforced by the community of the faithful, we find that *as a group* we offer ourselves to God without concern for our own self-love. This escape from self-centeredness may last for only brief moments within the period of worship, but when the escape is to the reality of the living God, we take a step toward greater wholeness of personality.

The chief way in which the Church speaks to its members is symbols. Symbols are mirrors of divine power. They point beyond themselves to the ultimate reality of God, and we learn to look through them and to see the living God. They become the means whereby the divine power of God becomes active in us. Joan of Arc was trembling with fear when facing death, and yet when a soldier placed a rough cross in her hands, she found the courage to face the agony of fire with triumphant faith.

The Church is rich in such symbols. The meaning of the Cross is not self-evident, but it grows in significance as we become immersed in the Gospel story. Bread and wine are the most common of foods, but they gain uncommon meaning because of the use of them by Jesus at the Last Supper and by the centuries of tradition in the Church. Water, as the symbol of inward cleansing, had one meaning for the followers of John the Baptist and another for the early Christians, and it comes down the ages as the means whereby we are made into new creatures.

Symbolism may become dangerous when specific acts, words, and pictures become ends in themselves. They are open to the magical uses of the superstitious, and therefore provide only an *ersatz* answer to anxiety. But at the same time, few people worship effectively without some symbols, and it is likely that the avoidance of traditional symbols may lead to a new kind of symbolism, as in the use that the Society of Friends make of silence.

Worshiping together with the use of symbols demands participation on the part of the congregation. We do not go to church as we do to a concert or a lecture, although quite properly anthems and the spoken word are part of worship. In this respect, it is not accurate to speak of a worshiping group as an "audience," for although they are "hearers," they are faced with the dictum of the letter of James: "Be ye doers of the word, and not hearers only" (1:22, KJ); "obey the message; do not merely listen to it, and deceive yourselves" (G). The genius of Christian worship has always required the congregation to participate in the hymns, chants, prayers, and action.

The sermon, also, if it is truly a proclamation of the Gospel, is a stimulus to our faith and demands a response. It places before the minds of the worshipers new insights into the nature of belief, new reasons for the faith that is in them, and new interpretations of the meaning of worship. It confronts them with Jesus Christ and is a means of grace whereby they may respond to the gifts that God offers them. The sermon is backed by the Holy Scriptures, which is the basis for our faith.

Second, corporate worship deepens the emotional resources of Christian behavior. The architecture of the church provides a primary emotional response. Although we may prefer modern, colonial, Gothic, or some other kind of architecture, we find in any church the structure and the symbols that make us respond with an act of reverence.

The music in worship speaks primarily to the emotions.

From the organ prelude through the hymns, canticles, responses, and anthems to the postlude, the music is affecting our muscles and glands as well as our minds. Music is soothing or exciting or melodious or discordant. The words are coordinated with the tune to provide a meaningful whole, and these combinations produce emotional effects that may be good or bad, depending on both aspects.

Corporate prayer is always a source of power when rightly conceived. Confession leads to spiritual cleansing; absolution leads to a sense of well-being; aspiration and intercession focusses the attention on the needs of others; thanksgiving causes one to take stock of his blessings; and adoration carries one into a sense of awe and reverence before the Most High. But, chiefly, the attitude of prayer itself, when supported by the contagion of the common aspirations of the congregation, provides a sense of personal relationship with the living God.

Third, common worship reinforces and directs the will of the worshipers. This is not accomplished, however, by isolating the will from man's other attributes. Worship affects the whole man, and thus provides a renewed sense of integration centering in a personal God. In the relationship of worship, the total personality is strengthened and redirected by the power of the Holy Spirit.

Public worship satisfies the whole man. It deepens his commitment and renews his spirit. He finds new sources of energy whereby he is enabled to overcome temptation, to forgive those who have offended against him, and to restore his relationships with those from whom he has been alienated. As a result, his own vocation as a witness to the love of Christ is made clearer, and he finds it easier to be obedient to the leading of the Holy Spirit.

There is a difference between religious and non-religious

people, and it comes out primarily in the effects of genuine worship on our daily lives. Dr. Pratt, who had unusually good opportunities to observe the effects of all religions, put it in clear and simple terms:

The typically religious people I have known give the impression of not having all their eggs in one basket; or, if they have, that basket is in some realm where thieves do not break through nor steal. They refuse to take the chances and changes of their immediate fate too seriously. They possess a certain quiet calm and a certain inner joy through all the drudgery of the common day. And in the hour of trial their faces are often radiant. They had prepared themselves for just such moments. In short, I find in religious people a certain depth, a certain stability which, in non-religious people of corresponding native equipment, I fail to discern.[3]

Why, then, do people go to church? The primary reason is a very simple one: *they go to church because they expect to meet God there.* They do not go to play psychological tricks on themslves, or to feel good, or to improve their health, or even to seek salvation, although these may be by-products of religion.

"To worship," said William Temple,

is to quicken the conscience by the holiness of God, to feed the mind with the truth of God, to purge the imagination with the beauty of God, to open the heart to the love of God, to devote the will to the purpose of God. All this is gathered up in that emotion which most cleanses us from selfishness because it is the most selfless of all emotions—adoration.[4]

We go to church, then, to enlist in the army of God, and, when we have enlisted, to serve. God becomes our King whom we adore. In all the facets of corporate worship at its best, we discover God at work to give us the benefits of his grace: reinforced faith, forgiveness of sins, emotions of blessedness and peace, strength renewed to do his will. There is no place except in the common worship of believers where we may expect this to occur. An invitation is open to everyone of us to

> Seek the LORD while he may be found,
> Call upon him while he is near.
> (Isaiah 55:6, G)

An anonymous hymn reminds us that we are not helpless in our seeking, for there is a prior act of God that makes it possible for us to turn to him.

> I sought the Lord, and afterward I knew
> He moved my soul to seek him, seeking me;
> It was not I that found, O Saviour true;
> No, I was found of thee.[5]

This sense of God who seeks us in and through the community is unknown to the person who is anxious and alone. For the anxious person stands outside the Church, looking for a moral code that will make him acceptable. Charles R. Stinnette, Jr., writes that

his troubled mind seeks those fruits of Christianity that he cannot have, unless he is willing to take his place in the life-giving plant, which is the Church. The gifts of the Holy Spirit will belong to man again when he comes out of his barracaded isolation into the community of faith and expectancy. He that stands outside and demands salvation will never know the spontaneity of a love that rejoices in hope and is 'patient in tribulation.' . . . Christian faith does not end with forgiveness of sins nor with relief from anxiety. It incorporates man into an ongoing transcendent community of the forgiven and the forgiving, where in moments of faith and love he lives beyond anxiety. Thus the Church through her life and sacraments provides healing for the tragic anxiety of existence.[6]

## THE LORD'S SUPPER

Symbol and adoration reach their highest level in the Lord's Supper. Although worship in terms of prayer, Scripture, and sermon is the most common of our forms, the Lord's Supper has always been the central act of the congregation. It has been played down in some denominations because it is a sacred meal, and it has been played up in others for the same reason, but Christians have always agreed on its significance.

The invitation is often thought of in terms of spiritual thirst. "If any man thirst, let him come to me, and drink" (John 7:37, RSV), is the way it is expressed in the Fourth Gospel. This is reminiscent of the second Isaiah when he sang:

> Ho! everyone that is thirsty, come to the waters,
> And he that has no money, come buy, and eat. . . .
> Incline your ear, and come to me,
> Listen, that you may live!    (Isaiah 55:1,3, G)

The invitation is offered to all. It is the promise of an oasis while one is crossing the desert stretches of life. And we respond by saying, "I was glad when they said unto me, We will go into the house of the Lord" (Psalm 122:1, PB).

The one who offers this invitation is the living Christ, who is our host. We sing,

> Come, risen Lord, and deign to be our guest;
> Nay, let us be thy guests; the feast is thine;
> Thyself at thine own board make manifest
> In this our Sacrament of Bread and Wine.[7]

Let us be honest with ourselves. We have no resources for abundant living, for salvation, for freedom from care and worry. We have no resources, that is, within ourselves. Every day, in the routine of living, we face obstacles and frustrations that we cannot solve alone. We talk over our problems with our friends; we stop work for a coffee break; we need our loved ones. We find ourselves saying with the Psalmist:

Like as the hart desireth the water-brooks, so
longeth my soul after thee, O God.
My soul is athirst for God, yea, even for the
living God.          (Psalm 42:1,2a, PB)

In the Fourth Gospel, there is a story of Jesus and the
woman by the well. As they talked, Jesus referred to "living
water," and this confused the woman. So Jesus said, "Anyone
who drinks of this water will be thirsty again, but anyone who
drinks the water that I will give him will never be thirsty, but
the water that I will give him will become a spring of water
within him, bubbling up for eternal life" (John 4:14, G).

This refreshing and strengthening power of God's grace is
available to all who have faith in him, but it is channeled particularly through Christian worship and above all in Holy
Communion.

We, who know so well that our bodies must be supplied
with food and water, forget that our total persons need nourishment in the same regular way. When the weather gets hot, we
need to take care that we will not run out of water, but we
know that our general health depends on constant use of God's
provender.

Henry Sloane Coffin, writing in the reformed tradition,
brought out the three elements held in common among Protestants: First, "Christ himself presides at his table," the minister representing both Christ and the people in this action.
Second, "through the sacramental action that which is symbol-
ized becomes a blessed reality by the power of the Spirit to those
who partake in faith." Third, "Through the entire sacramental
action, . . . Christ communicates himself." It is a commemo-
ration of Christ's sacrifice, in which we present ourselves as "a
living sacrifice." [8] This is brought out in John Brownlie's hymn:

Let thy blood in mercy poured,
Let thy gracious body broken,
Be to me, O gracious Lord,
Of thy boundless love the token:
Thou didst give thyself for me;
Now I give myself to thee.[9]

As we make a self-offering of ourselves at the Lord's Table, we are drawn into the drama of Christ's sacrifice on the cross. Sometimes we are carried back to the Last Supper and find that we are identified with this twelve at the holy feast. At other times, we may feel drawn into the community of the saints throughout the centuries, who by giving themselves to Christ made this world a province of the kingdom of God. Or, it is I alone who goes to the communion rail, and I am identified with the living Christ in the communion of bread and wine.

Thou didst give thyself for me;
Now I give myself to thee.

Christ is present at his table, prior to the faith of the Church or of the communicant. But he is received by us through our faith. The whole act of communion is the corporate action of the Church, and the various churches provide their own discipline, ministry, and order whereby the Lord's Supper may be celebrated, but it must never be forgotten that it is a feast at which Christ is the host. It is *his* meal and *not ours*.

In his *Small Catechism,* Martin Luther asked how bodily eating and drinking can do such wondrous things. His answer was:

It is not the eating and drinking indeed that does it, but the words which stand here, 'Given and shed for you, for the remission of sins.' These words, together with the bodily eating and drinking, are the chief thing in the Sacrament; and he that believes these words, has what they say and mean, namely the forgiveness of sins.

Who then receives this Sacrament worthily? Fasting and bodily preparation are indeed a good outward discipline; but he is truly worthy and well prepared who has faith in these words: 'Given and shed for you, for the remission of sins.' But he who believes not these words, or doubts, is unworthy and unprepared; for the words, 'For you,' require only believing hearts.[10]

To what may be likened this refreshment of the Lord's Supper? It is like a glass of fruit juice in the middle of the afternoon, when children come home from school fatigued by the tensions of classroom work. For in that liquid there is refreshment of body and soul, and in that act there is the loving gift of a mother. It is like a friend dropping in when we are tired or lonely or ill, for there is refreshment in fellowship. It is like being alone on a mountain top, drinking in the beauties of nature and breathing the clear, cool air, and yet knowing that you are not alone. It is like the caress of a wife, with its trust and love, for God's presence is a token of his care for us. It is as common as bread and wine, as lowly as the death of a criminal on a cross, as simple as the gathering of all sorts and conditions of men. It is as rare as martyrdom, as expensive as the death of God's unique Son, as self-giving as God's love for us. It is like all these, but it is much more. It is a refreshment that is like nothing else that man can experience, for it is God's gift of himself, through Christ, to us under the forms of bread and wine. The Lord's Supper is an outward and visible sign of an inward and spiritual grace, made available to us through the life and death and resurrection of God's Son, our Redeemer who says, "Come unto me, and I will refresh you."

"Come unto me," is a gracious invitation. It is a call to everyone of us, especially those who are weary or burdened or distressed. "Ho! everyone that is thirsty, come to the waters." "If any man thirst, let him come to me, and drink."

# CHAPTER FOURTEEN

# How the Church Helps

The claim that our fundamental needs are met by the Church is one that outsiders do not normally accept, and often casual church members discover that they do not find life meaningful as a result of attending church. This is because of two basic misunderstandings: we do not comprehend our true needs, and we do not know what the Church really is.

The sense of insecurity and lostness, the feeling of lawlessness and moral confusion, the frustration of trying to make decisions, and the loss of the awareness of God's nearness may be overcome by life in the Church. But this depends on an understanding of what the Church has to offer.

We crave to be loved and accepted, and we may know in our minds that only as we love and accept others is it possible for them to love and accept us. Yet none of us is capable of consistent self-giving. We find distrust and suspicion all around us, and our relationships with others are broken. The Church at its best offers us this love and acceptance without any reservations, and it provides the assurance that God loves us and makes it possible for members of the congregation to love each other.

We need a structure of law and order. Much of our drifting and moral confusion is because we have lost the sense of God's dependableness and justice. Even when we recognize the authority of law, we discover that we cannot obey the law. Our helplessness before the demands of the law lead to despair. The Church at its best offers us an interpretation of the universe based on natural and moral law, and provides the means whereby our own lives may have structure and meaning.

Every impulse in us is toward growth. We desire to be free to grow in our total persons. The tragedy of life is that growth is frustrated at every level, or else it goes in the wrong direction. If a tree is to bear fruit, it must be watered and pruned; and if a man is to grow in grace, he needs both nourishment of the spirit and guidance from outside himself. The Church at its best provides the means of grace as both growth and guidance as God uses the community of the faithful to support and assist all its members.

Each of us senses the mystery of life and demands some interpretation of the ultimate mystery behind all the meanings we can discover. There is wonder in the face of the unknown, but there is also the tremendous amount of knowledge that has opened up the mysteries of the atom and of time and space. This sense of the mysterious may be satisfied by superstition, magic, or even by denial that it exists. As Paul said in his sermon to the Athenians:

Men of Athens, from every point of view I see that you are extremely religious. For as I was going about and looking at the things you worship, I even found an altar with this inscription: 'To an unknown God.' So it is that what you already worship in ignorance I am now telling you of. (Acts 17:23-24, G)

The Church at its best tells us the truth about the mystery of God. In Jesus Christ is found "the way, the truth, and the life," and this is "the truth" that "shall make you free."

## WHAT IS THE CHURCH?

The historic Church seeks to become the kind of fellowship that meets man's basic needs for acceptance, law, growth, and outreach toward the ultimate mystery. Not every congregation achieves this, and the institutional structure of what we call a "church" is not this "true" Church. The "true" Church is a divine-human society that was founded by God through Jesus Christ, and one dwells in this fellowship through faith. It is a fellowship in which all the members know themselves to be sinners in need of forgiveness, and therefore they are willing to forgive others in the fellowship. It is this communion of persons under God which is the "true" Church.

There is only one place where we can find this "true" Church, and that is in the local parish. A particular congregation may give few signs of being a community of the Holy Spirit, but the possibility of being such a community is always present in the smaller groups of people who have caught the vision of what the Church ought to be.

Within the fellowship of the living Christ, our basic needs are met. Our ultimate requirement for love and acceptance is met by showing us the forgiving love of God in Christ. The teachings of the Church point to the moral law as found in Scripture and in the Christian conscience. The requirements for justice and social righteousness, the threat of judgment on sinful men and nations, the prophetic hope of a Messiah, and the simple summary that we must "do justice, and love kindness, and walk humbly with God" are found in the Scriptures. The freedom and direction of our growth depends on our response in faith within the community to the grace of God, for it is by God's grace that we become "worthy of the vocation to which we are called." Within the Church, we discover that we are worshiping a God who has removed some of the mystery of his being through the events of history by which he is revealed to us.

When one comes to Christian maturity, he not only knows these things, but he has reached that stage whereby he assimilates these truths into his total personality. His anxieties are destroyed, save for the ultimate anxiety that he will never be worthy of the love so freely given to him.

## WHAT THE CHURCH DOES

The local Church shares in the life of the "true" Church when the redemptive love of God is at work among its members. The functions of the local parish are for the purpose of strengthening the fellowship of the faithful in their relations with their fellows and with God.

### 1. Worship

The worshiper is seeking the true God, who will pardon him for his sins and restore the right relationship between himself and his fellows, as well as between himself and God. This relationship is on higher terms than that of human justice. God is mighty, the Creator of all, who stands above and beyond the historical process, although he is also the Lord of history. God is working his purpose out, and we stand in awe before him. This reverence is the beginning of wisdom as well as of worship.

When we go to church, we expect to meet God there. We find the God who works through our anxieties so that we are enabled to seek first the kingdom of God and his righteousness.

We come into a personal relationship with him "who is a very present help in trouble," who lifts us up and turns us in new directions, and who calls us to new forms of service.

Worship is always communion and proclamation. We come into the house of the Lord. But we listen to him while we are in his presence. The significance of preaching is that it is always a retelling of what God has done for us. It is the good news of the Gospel, seen as a full-fledged drama of God's acts in history for our redemption. When the Gospel is proclaimed, it is always proclaimed *for us,* and therefore what is preached must be relevant to today's world.

Sometimes a distinction is made between preaching and teaching in the New Testament. Proclamation and telling are considered by some to be two different things. But just as no preaching is Christian unless it relates the biblical revelation to our times, so no teaching is Christian unless it relates the story of God's acts in history to the learners of today. The saving truth of the Gospel is mediated through personality in both the pulpit and classroom.

But preaching has its peculiar dimension. We are preaching for a decision! We are preaching to create faith! We are preaching Christ crucified and risen again for our salvation. Through the words of the preacher we expect to hear the Word of the Lord. This does not always happen, and when it fails to occur our worship is short-circuited. But even in poor preaching, we can listen for the Word that God holds out to us through the grace of human words.

In worship, we come before the Lord as sinners needing forgiveness, as believers who know that because Christ died, our redemption is possible; as listeners to the Word of God revealed in the mighty acts of God recorded in the Bible and interpreted in the sermon; as men who affirm their faith in creeds or hymns; as those who express their "soul's sincere desire" in terms of "not my will, but thine be done." As we come into Christ's presence at his Supper, we find refreshment for our souls. We place our anxieties and frustrations and sins at God's altar, and through the ministry of reconciliation we find that God restores us to relationship with him.

## 2. Fellowship

The Church is a fellowship of *persons,* or it is nothing. The Holy Spirit was given to the *community.* The recognition of being unworthy in God's sight leads us to need the support of others who have the same burden. At this point, a change takes place. Wayne E. Oates has described it as follows:

The shrinking lonely ones turn and seek community with those who will understand from experience the real change that has taken place. The result of this movement of persons who have partaken of the sufferings of Jesus Christ is a fellowship of suffering and a fellowship of concern. The participants bear one another's burden and so fulfill the law of Christ. Those who have been comforted of God become a comfort to those who are in any affliction by means of the comfort with which they themselves have been comforted of God.[1]

The "true" Church is always such a redemptive congregation. It is a congregation of sinners needing redemption, but it is also a congregation of those who are practicing a ministry of reconciliation. The spirit of Christ works through them to renew their minds and in their transformation is seen their deeper loyalty to the will of God.

This was true of the primitive Church, often in an exciting way. Their sense of community was so strong that at one time all property was held in common, and there was a common treasury from which each received what was needed. The con-

cern for widows and orphans, which the letter of James identified with "pure religion and undefiled," led to the appointment
of seven men as deacons in charge of the accounts. The love
feast preceding the Lord's Supper emphasized the sharing of
food before the sharing of the Lord's presence. They were concerned with those who fell by the wayside and sought to re-
claim them for the fellowship.

### 3. Instruction

The Church is concerned that its members receive *instruction* in Christian truth. This, in turn, depends on the quality
of life in the worship and fellowship of the local congregation.
When a parish worships in such a way that every worshiper is
worshiping the Father in spirit and in truth, and when the fellowship is such that we can say, "Behold how these Christians
love one another," we have an atmosphere in which Christian
education may take place. Without such an atmosphere, there
may be instruction in factual knowledge about the history and
beliefs of the Church, but it will not help children or adults to
grow in the nurture and admonition of the Lord.

Christian education takes place when the learner's basic
needs are met and when his fundamental questions are answered in terms of the Gospel. This occurs within a spiritual
environment of true worship and the redemptive life.

The fundamental questions people ask by attitudes or words
are the same from infancy to old age. We are always asking,
"Who am I?" "Who are you?" "Where did I come from?"
"What is the world like?" "Where are we going?" Christian
education takes place when these questions are answered in
terms of the relationships we have with people and with God.

In this way, we begin to appropriate to ourselves the truth
that sets us free from anxiety, and therefore we discover the

perfect love that casts out fear. This kind of instruction is possible in the "true" Church which is a fellowship of the Holy Spirit.

Such instruction as this is always part of the minister's task. The ordination service in the *Book of Common Prayer* includes this question: "Are you persuaded that the Holy Scriptures contain all Doctrine required as necessary for eternal salvation through faith in Jesus Christ? And are you determined, out of the said Scriptures to instruct the people committed to your charge; and to teach nothing, as necessary to eternal salvation, but that which you shall be persuaded may be concluded and proved by the Scriptures?" This teaching ministry may take place from the pulpit, as we have already indicated, but it is a constant element in the vocation of the person ordained.

The church school teacher shares this same ministry, for there is a priesthood of all believers. The important element in the make-up of a teacher is that he has a faith to be shared. The proclamation of this faith may never take the form of preaching in a technical sense, but education for Christian living is always education for redemption. "This child," says the church school teacher, "is one for whom Christ died. He has come to this church and to me looking for a faith by which to live meaningfully *now*. What have I to give him?" And the only answer, ultimately, is that the teacher may become a channel for the working of the Holy Spirit, so that God's grace may lead this child into increased wisdom and faith.

## 4. Pastoral Work

The pastoral concern of the Church reaches all of its members. When Jesus was asked who he was, he replied, "The blind are regaining their sight, the lame can walk, the lepers are being cured and the deaf can hear, the dead are being raised up and the good news is being preached to the poor" (Luke 7:22, G).

The clergy are the professionals in pastoral work, trained to meet people's needs by their spiritual insight and psychological skills. They excel in these tasks because of their pastoral and counseling procedures. They make themselves accessible to all members of the congregation. They are shepherds who care for their sheep in the name of the Good Shepherd. This relationship of the Christian to his pastor provides one of the great opportunities for achieving mental and spiritual health through the means that God has provided.

But the pastoral work of the Church is not restricted to the clergy. Lay people have a similar responsibility. When the worshiping congregation is truly a redemptive and sustaining community where God's grace is channeled through the members for the sake of each other, the cares of each become the cares of all. In times of emergency, sickness, tragedy, and death, the members of the congregation minister to the suffering and the needy. The self-giving love of God is given to persons through persons, and thus the lost are found and the spiritually dead come to life again.

## 5. Missionary Motive

The Church functions throughout the world because of its missionary motive. All that we have said about the Church is voided unless the missionary motive is strong. The Good News of Jesus Christ cannot be acquired by anyone unless he is willing to share it. The Gospel cannot be placed in a capsule of an individual's faith or of a parish's activities. It is the kind of news that has to be shouted from the housetops in order to be assimilated into one's life.

The Church has always understood this. For the Gospels and Epistles to be intelligible, the New Testament story needs the *Acts of the Apostles,* with its account of the spread of the Gospel throughout the known world. The story of Pentecost is the report of the gift of the Holy Spirit to others than the disciples. Every one of Paul's letters was written to a congregation founded because of the missionary motive. The dramatic expansion of the Church across Africa and Europe in the early centuries was due to the fact that the nitroglycerine of the Gospel is too hot to handle unless it is shared.

In our genuine appreciation of the early Church, we are likely to forget that the greatest expansion of Christianity took place in the nineteenth century! We are living today on the momentum of a tremendous missionary movement, and the Church has an outpost today in almost every country in the world. Christ died for the redemption of *all* mankind.

The unerring spiritual logic of the Church has always been, *"Share the good news or die."* To go into all the world and preach the Gospel is both a command for action and a requirement for a mature spiritual life. The joy of bringing one's fellows to Christ is a reward beyond all description. We do not do this in order to overcome our anxiety, but in the self-forgetfulness of missionary endeavor anxiety is banished.

## 6. Beyond Nationalism

The final function of the Church is its supranational relationships. While there are national churches, the "true" Church always transcends national boundaries. This is evident today in the World Council of Churches, which draws representatives from the nations of the entire non-Roman Catholic world to its meetings.

In the primitive Church, this Christian loyalty that went beyond national allegiance was obvious, for the Christian martyrs were willing to accept any punishment rather than bow to the pressure of worshiping the emperor. Christians in Rome, Corinth, and Jerusalem were brothers, no matter what racial background they may have had. There was no distinction between the dark-skinned Egyptians and the dark-haired Jewish Christians and the Romans and Greeks. There was neither barbarian nor Scythian, for all were one in Christ. This supranational loyalty is caught in John Oxenham's hymn,

> Join hands, then, brothers of the faith,
> Whate'er your race may be,
> Who serves my Father as a son
> Is surely kin to me.[2]

There were arguments in the Church from the beginning, however, and it was not long before there were different organizations. This destructive trend toward separation continued through the centuries until the reversal began in 1910 with a conference in Edinburgh, and now there are more mergers of denominations and grounds for fellowship than in many centuries.

Two examples of the Church at work in recent years show how the Church crosses national lines. Members of the American Friends Service Commission have been able to operate behind the lines of the enemy in recent wars because of their obvious loyalty to Christ and their fellowship with all men. The World Council of Churches was able to keep open channels of communication at all times during World War II and to bring to the needy the gifts of Christian love immediately after hostilities ceased. Loyalty to God remains greater than loyalty to Caesar.

## *YOU NEED THE CHURCH*

As we look at the needs that you have, as we look at the real nature of the Church, as we see what the Church at its best does, it becomes more and more obvious that *you* need the Church.

You need the Church because it is the only genuine fellowship interested in bringing about, by God's grace, the development of your total personality against the background of your basic needs.

You need the Church because it is the only community that channels God's grace through its sacraments and worship for the purpose of making a new person out of you.

You need the Church because it is a fellowship of the Holy Spirit, where Christ is the agent of your redemption.

You need the Church because through its worship you are meeting God in the presence of his congregation.

You need the Church because through its fellowship you know yourself to be loved and accepted as you are.

You need the Church because only in such a community can you receive the Christian education that is true nurture in the Christian way of living.

You need the Church because it ministers to you and provides many opportunities for you to minister to others.

You need the Church because your faith can be kept alive and grace can come to you only as you seek to give your faith to others through the missionary work of the Church.

You need the Church because it is the only organization that crosses national boundaries and provides a loyalty big enough to bring peace on earth among men of good will.

In the Church you will find the Good News of Jesus Christ,

and in him is the hope of our salvation. Through the life of the "true" Church you will find that your basic needs are met and your fundamental questions are answered on a level deep enough to provide stability and maturity in a world where all else might crumble. The "true" Church is a *community of love,* and "there is no fear in love, but perfect love casts out fear" (I John 4:18, RSV).[3]

# PART V

# FACING OUR TROUBLES

# CHAPTER FIFTEEN

# When Life Seems Hard

A world without any troubles in it would be a mighty sorry one. Doctors would have no patients, lawyers would have no clients, plumbers would have no emergency calls, fire engines would rust, the police would be fired, and most of us would be starved for conversation. But what would make such a problem serious is that none of us would have any troubles to overcome, and therefore we could cease to grow. Life would contain no challenges; there would be no tensions in living, no zest, no flavor.

When a man in good health retires at the age of 65, unless he has enough hobbies to challenge him with real problems, he is likely to enter a period of rapid deterioration. He cannot find anything to do, any problems to solve, any obstacles to overcome. He becomes restless and seeks an outlet in recreation, or he becomes a complainer and a semi-invalid, or he quits living and dies.

Life is always a series of problems, and we grow as we meet and surmount difficulties. Where there are no tensions, no conflicts, and no obstacles, there is no stimulus to make us grow. We place exercise bars before little children so that they can develop their muscles; we provide problems adequate for young minds in our educational systems; we try to challenge brilliant students with more difficult studies. Obstacle courses are standard procedures in military training. This same principle applies through all of life, and the retired person finds meaning in life only when he can discover something that challenges him. He needs to do more than "occupy his time."

All of this applies only to a "tolerable amount" of trouble. Our problems frequently seem to become burdens we cannot shoulder or cast off. When such difficulties begin to break down our morale, when they culminate in evil and suffering, when life seems hard and no answer appears on the horizon, we are ready to sing, "I'm gonna tell God all of my troubles."

When we become anxious about such troubles, they seem even more unbearable. There are a number of ways of meeting, accepting, and overcoming them.

## FACING OUR TROUBLES

The first thing to do with any difficulty is to face it squarely. Few men faced as many problems as Abraham Lincoln. A story is told that one day he was striding down the street with his two boys, both of whom were crying. "Why, Mr. Lincoln, what's the matter with them?" asked a friend. "Just what's the matter with the whole world," replied Lincoln. "I've got three walnuts and each wants two."

Facing problems squarely reduces them to their own dimensions, and thus they do not grow in our imaginations, do not fester human relations, and do not seem insurmountable. To know the problem in some cases is to know the answer. That is why telling one's troubles to a trusted pastor is important; it puts the problem in the right perspective and thus clarifies the whole point at issue.

Another story about Lincoln is pertinent. Secretary Stanton was angry with one of his officers and he told Lincoln that he was going to write him and give him a piece of his mind. Lincoln encouraged him to do this and when the letter was finished Stanton asked by whom he could send it.

"Send it?" Lincoln replied. "Why don't send it at all. Tear it up. You have freed your mind on the subject, and that is all that is necessary. Tear it up. You never want to send such letters. I never do."

The important factor was that Stanton's thoughts were not repressed, not pushed back into his subconscious where they would pop up again. He expressed them, got them out of his system, and then he could forget about them. Human relations are often soothed by such a method. The Church offers the same catharsis through prayers of confession, by which we pour out our thoughts, problems, and admission of sin to a forgiving God of love.

But this is only one way of facing a problem. Our troubles are frequently too stubborn to be eliminated by talking them out. If a person thinks he is sick, he may become sick by haboring the thought. A doctor's examination may show that he is perfectly well, and if he is mature he will accept this diagnosis. But he may really be physically ill, and facing the facts may involve facing an operation, special medication, or adjustment to a slower pace in life. It pays to know the facts in any case, for then we can deal with our problems realistically.

> He who would valiant be
> 'Gainst all disaster,
> Let him in constancy
> Follow the Master.
> There's no discouragement
> Shall make him once relent

His first avowed intent
To be a pilgrim.[1]

The resources of Christian faith help us to face the facts with a certain heroism, and like the swimmer suffering the agony of anticipation because the water is cold, it is not bad when he starts to swim.

## MISERY LOVES COMPANY

A strange quirk in the human animal is that misery loves company. It is a solace to know that someone is in a worse spot than we are.

There is an old story of a man who went to a magician or sorcerer and asked that his troubles be taken from him. The wizard answered that if he toured the country and found anybody with no troubles at all, he would lift this man's difficulties from him. As time went on, the man became desperate because everyone had troubles; but by the time he was through, he became convinced that his own problems were minor compared with those of other people. He returned to the magician with his report, and made no request about his own troubles.

Misery loves company for two reasons: the discovery that many people are more unfortunate than we are puts our own problems in perspective, and talking with others about their problems leads to a mutual healing and strengthening power.

## PUT PROBLEMS ASIDE

Some of us have the wonderful capacity to forget about our problems. We can put them aside and work on something that promises more fruitful results. Later on, we may come back to the original problem—if it is still there.

This is not an easy thing to learn, however, because often our anxiety lies in exactly this: we keep all our problems with us all of the time. Horatio Dresser once listed the kinds of fears that surround us:

There is a long line of particular fears and trouble-bearing expectations: such . . . as ideas associated with certain articles of food, the dread of the east wind, terrors of hot weather, aches and pains associated with cold weather, fear of catching cold if one sits in a draft, the coming of hay fever on the fourteenth of August. . . . Yet this is not all. This vast array is swelled by innumerable volunteers from daily life: fear of accident, possibility of calamity, loss of property, chance of robbery, fire, or war. And it is not deemed sufficient to fear for ourselves. When a friend is taken ill, we must forthwith fear the worst and apprehend death. . . . There is an ocean of morbidity.[2]

Such fears are normal, but they are not Christian. They fit into what George Hedley calls "the superstitions of the irreligious." They are dramatically illustrated by baseball players who have many little quirks, by auto-racing drivers who tie baby shoes to their front springs, by all kinds of people with little fears and superstitions that rule their lives.

Christian faith is a means of putting our troubles aside, of overcoming our fears. It means not enlarging our problems by means of undue worry. We sing that God says,

Fear not, I am with thee; O be not dismayed!
For I am thy God and will still give thee aid;
I'll strengthen thee, help thee, and cause thee to stand,
Upheld by my righteous, omnipotent hand.[3]

## HANDICAPS

It helps also to look at our troubles as handicaps. A handicap is always something to be overcome. A golfer with a handicap is expected to overcome that difficulty and win his match. A horse with a handicap of carrying extra weight is presumed to be able to defeat lesser horses with lighter weights. A steeplechase has barriers to challenge the best horses and riders, and no one can win by riding around them. When handicaps seem particularly difficult, they become as challenges to be met.

A well known clergyman once visited a hospital for soldiers and sailors who had lost either their arms or legs. He stood in the middle of the ward, where everyone could see him, and began to take off his clothes. He showed them the brace that supported his back, he took off a shoe and showed them a deformed foot, and he held out a hand that lacked several fingers. Then he limped around the room and let them look at him. It was a lesson they all remembered as they took their first difficult steps and learned the intricacies of artificial limbs and hands.

Harriet Houser's story of how her son accepted the complete immobilization of a broken neck and faced what was left of his life with cheerfulness and meaning illustrates the power of the spirit when it has deep religious resources.[4] I have known people with incurable diseases who continued to live to the full for many months or years. They accepted their fate without bitterness, because they saw it as a handicap that they could live with.

There are permanent disabilities such as blindness, deafness, and lameness. Many people live with these handicaps with such deep meaning that we wonder at the glories of compensation that God has placed at man's disposal. While God may grow missing tails on some animals, he provides spiritual resources by which man works through his handicaps.

## *RECONCILIATION*

God also gives us grace to become reconciled to our troubles. This does not mean giving up hope or admitting defeat. It means being restored to harmony, being pacified or adjusted, or simply being made friendly. We learn to live with ourselves as we are.

Humor is often necessary for this kind of perspective. Junius Brutus Booth, the actor, had a broken nose. A gushing admirer was talking with him and said, "You're such a wonderful actor, but to be perfectly frank, I can't get over your nose." "Can't get over my nose?" he replied. "Of course not, the bridge is broken."

The strangest thing about Christian faith is that when believers become reconciled to their weaknesses, God makes them strong. Paul was aware of this and drew from his own experience. He had what he called "a thorn in the flesh," "a physical handicap" (P). He wrote,

Three times I besought the Lord about this, that it should leave me; but he said to me, 'My grace is sufficient for you, for my power is made perfect in weakness.' I will all the more gladly boast of my weaknesses, that the power of Christ may rest upon me. For the sake of Christ, then, I am content with weaknesses, insults, hardships, persecutions, and calamities; for when I am weak, then I am strong. (II Corinthians 12:8-10, RSV)

Paul's affliction may have been epilepsy or malaria, but whatever it was, it is clear that Paul became reconciled to it. He discovered that God could use his affliction for a better purpose. Many handicapped and crippled people have discovered that their limitations opened new channels for meaningful living. We see a new depth in character among those who have learned to live with their diseases, paralyses, or loss of specific

179

functions. It is the victory of reconciliation rather than the over-coming of the handicap that provides spiritual maturity.

## CHANGING LIFE'S SITUATIONS

We want to change life's situations, too. There are limit-ations that can be overcome; there are barriers to a well-adjusted, moral, and meaningful life that can be dismantled. Some of them are inside of us and others are put in our way by the out-side world. Being remade in the image of Christ, with power to move along the straight and narrow way that leads to the kingdom of God, is a motive built within us and never com-pletely destroyed by outside events. Remaking the world, getting rid of injustices, eliminating war, poverty and political corrup-tion, and making people's suffering and haunting fears un-necessary, are other motives that keep recurring in our subcon-scious minds.

Men of good will have always sought to make this world a better one. Although many of our anxieties rise up from the inside, it is obvious that social conditions contribute to our wor-ries and our fears. When Walter Rauschenbusch walked among the slum homes of his parishoners, he realized that when men were struggling for morsels of bread they did not have time to hear of the living bread of the Gospel. Changed conditions mean changed lives. Ministers in modern suburbia and exurbia run into the same condition in reverse: life is so comfortable and isolated from the tensions of living that the Gospel seems irrelevant, and then new conditions arise and suburbanites and exurbanites have difficulty discovering the relevance of the Gos-pel to the new kind of hecticness. There are some new sub-divisions in which churches are barred because they might hurt property values!

Many people throw themselves into social and moral reform activities in order to escape from their own problems. This rarely works out, as the result normally is to place one's anxieties under the thin veneer of a vaguely defined social consciousness. The distraught mother who spends so much time in the PTA that her own children are neglected is a shining example of such a failure.

The self-forgetfulness that comes from being engaged in social activities, however, turns our thoughts outward and provides a means for overcoming our anxieties. The sense of mission that results from participation in church activities often leads to a new perspective on one's own problems and therefore contributes to the changing of that situation as well as to the performance of community responsibilities.

When our problems are faced squarely, we find in the community resources that assist us in overcoming them. The Church, with its pastoral and counseling functions, is one of the primary sources for this guidance. The sources of power, as God's grace is channeled through the life and worship of the Church, tap unexpected energy in ourselves, and we find that the combination of new personal power and the enveloping strength of the community of the faithful is enough to set our problems in such a perspective that we can overcome them.

### TRANSCENDING OUR TROUBLES

Christian faith may help us to face our troubles, to share them, to put them aside, to see them as handicaps, to be reconciled to them, or to overcome them, but it always provides the resources to transcend them.

The story is told of a little girl who was taken to visit Abraham Lincoln. She had heard that Lincoln was ugly. He took her on his knee and chatted with her in his merry way, and she turned to her father and said, "Oh, Daddy! He isn't ugly at all. He's just beautiful!" Such transcending of limitations is possible for those with greatness of soul.

Christian faith aids us in transcending our troubles. The Psalmist put it this way:

> O thou who hast made us see many dangers and disasters,
> Do thou quicken us again,
> And from the depths of the earth bring us up again.
> Do thou increase my greatness,
> And turn and comfort me!        (Psalm 71:20-21, G)

The Prophet of the exile taught thus:

> Whoever among you fears the LORD,
> And listens to the voice of his servant—
> Though he walk in darkness,
>     Without a gleam of light,
> Let him trust in the name of the LORD,
>     And rely on his God!
>                     (Isaiah 50:10, G)

Jesus gave us one of his most helpful sayings at this point:

> Come unto me, all of you who toil and are burdened (G)
>     that labor and are heavy laden (KJ)
>     that travail (PB)
> And I will refresh you (PB)
> I will give you rest (KJ)

Let my yoke be put upon you, and learn from me, for I am gentle and humble-minded, and your hearts will find rest, for the yoke I offer you is a kindly one, and the load I ask you to bear is light. (Matthew 11:28-30, G)

## GOD: FIRST OR LAST?

When our troubles are bad enough, we are likely to turn to God—after we have explored every other possibility. He is for many of us the last resort. After all our own efforts have failed, after the physician or psychiatrist has given up, we call for the minister and ask him to seek God as a last desperate effort to get things done the way we want.

Sometimes this works. But it is like asking a stranger for a favor. How many of us would ask an unknown person **for** the kind of favors we receive from intimate friends or parents? How many children turn to a stranger with the same confidence as they turn to their mothers or fathers?

It is not a fair deal to ask God to come in at the last moment to pull our fat out of the fire. It is true that because God loves us, it is never too late to turn to him, but we need to remind ourselves that God is not a stranger. God is our Father, who has acted throughout history to reveal himself to men and who has acted throughout our lives in love and justice. Therefore, it is our responsibility to keep in union with him even when life seems easy and without problems. We depend on him for every breath, and the whole creation is his. When we keep open the channels of communication, it is natural to ask God's help when life seems hard.

Such faith in God helps us to avoid the fatalism of the Stoics and the bitterness of the cynics, because we know he is a God of love. The Christian Gospel is an invitation to trust in God at all times, to keep in union with him through prayer and worship, and to know him through the community of the Holy Spirit in the local congregation. We discover that God is not a form of health insurance, not a guarantor of success in business, and not a magical guardian in times of danger. But he lifts us up to new heights, and gives us new perspective, and provides a radiance that makes life a joyful experience. He lifts men from the depths of despair and gives meaning to life even when what seems most precious has been taken away.

From these gifts of God comes that contagious enthusiasm for life that is living life abundantly. "Enthusiasm" means "in God" or "inspired." Eternal life becomes a quality of everyday living. To have such a victorious faith is to be "sure that neither death, nor life, . . . nor things present, nor things to come, . . . nor anything else in all creation, will be able to separate us from the love of God in Christ Jesus our Lord" (Romans 8:38-39, RSV).

This is the kind of serenity of faith of which Evelyn Cummins sings:

> I know not where the road will lead
> I follow day by day,
> Or where it ends: I only know
> I walk the King's highway.
>
> I know not if the road is long,
> And no one else can say;
> But rough or smooth, up hill or down,
> I walk the King's highway. . . .
>
> Through light and dark the road leads on
> Till dawns the endless day,
> When I shall know why in this life
> I walk the King's highway.[5]

# CHAPTER SIXTEEN

# Facing the Inevitable

From time to time, individuals and communities suffer from what are called natural calamities. The Litany, one of the historic services common to Lutherans, Episcopalians, and Roman Catholics, contains this petition:

> From lightning and tempest; from earthquake, fire,
> and flood; from plague, pestilence, and famine; from
> battle and murder, and from sudden death,
> *Good Lord, deliver us.*

This brings us to the question of God's relationship to natural law and our response to those forces of the universe that seem inexplicable and inevitable. The man under a tree who is struck by lightning, the utter destruction of an earthquake, the perils of fire and flood, the illness that strikes us in the prime of life, the death of a noble young soldier at the same time that a wastrel is untouched, death on the highways, and above all the death of a little child—all of these events occur as parts of our experience. Is life chaos? Or is natural law inhuman? Or is there a purpose behind all of this?

## GOD IS LOVE

"God is love, and he who abides in love abides in God, and God abides in him" (I John 4:16b, RSV). For love to be worth anything, it must be dependable. The constancy of God's love, by which we are saved, is expressed within a structure that is dependable and inevitable. God loves us, and we are capable of loving him. Yet God's love may seem to hurt us, and hurt us deeply and tragically, because of his dependableness.

God works according to what we call natural law. He has given us a dependable, consistent universe, and because God has chosen to reveal himself to us as love we believe that history and nature are essentially good. It is a world in which we are brought together in mutual love and understanding, in which the barriers that we have set up are broken down by means of his grace, and in which we can count on tomorrow's laws being the same as today's.

These laws, of course, are known to us only because of the consistency of events. No one ever saw a natural law, and we assume that because one event is connected with another that there is a cause and effect. What we call a natural law is a description of the dependableness of God's creation.

This kind of a universe is possible only if we are willing to take the consequences. There is a price to be paid for the non-personal consistency of natural law. When, according to natural law, the winds blow and the floods come, we must either meet the challenge with proper safeguards or take the consequences. When a drunken driver starts down the highway, the chances are increased that an accident will occur. An unknown virus may strike down a young mother. In such circumstances, a combination of natural factors leads to evil, and not any one natural law in itself.

When someone suffers or dies from the effects of natural law, I do *not* believe it is because God *wills* such results. I believe that God is dependable in his goodness and love, and that therefore he will not reverse his laws or suspend their operation to help us escape suffering. A mother might wish that her child would not be burned by touching a hot stove when a cake was being baked, but if God cooled the stove every time the child approached, it is obvious what would happen to the cake. God's world is consistent.

The Psalmist said it: "God . . . is a very present help in trouble" (Psalm 46:1, PB). No psalmist ever said, "God will take your troubles from you." We simply could not live in a world in which God reversed himself.

In the drama of Job in the Old Testament, Job had to discover this. He found out that Yahweh was not like Job, and that plague and famine and sudden death were parts of a righteous man's experience. Yahweh helped Job in his trouble, and Job came through his suffering with victory. He knew what Gerhardt Tersteegen envisioned:

> God himself is with us;
> Let us all adore him,
> And with awe appear before him.
> God is here within us,
> Soul, in silence fear him,
> Humbly, fervently draw near him.
> Now his own
> Who have known
> God, in worship lowly,
> Yield their spirits wholly.[1]

187

## DEATH

Death is the one inevitable experience. We may avoid the dangers of earthquake, fire, and flood, but the final experience of this life comes to all of us. Furthermore, death is good. Death comes to the aged and to the suffering as a release, and it is welcomed by them and often wished for by those who love them.

The process behind natural law leading to death is part of God's plan. Only when death comes at the wrong time is it evil. The *time* of death provides our evaluation of it. Premature death is due to a combination of natural laws, and from man's point of view it is due to chance. In our dependable universe, created by a loving God, there are unpredictable happenings. From the point of view of natural law, *after* they have occurred, they are events that are due to specific causes. But from the point of view of the persons who did not foresee or will them, these events seem to be sheer chance. A good God could not have willed this event directly, we say, and remained good. Yet we see that in this world created by a God of love, this kind of event occurs. It remains a mystery within the providence of Almighty God. God is so great that we cannot understand him.

The second Isaiah saw this. The sufferings of the nation as the kingdom was destroyed, as the land was devastated, and as the people were dispersed, were partially in terms of punishment because the people had disobeyed the moral law, but they were part of a larger plan. Yahweh had chosen Israel to receive his blessing and to be used for the redemption of the nations. This great prophet used the figure of a Suffering Servant who would save the nations to interpret God's love for his people in the midst of suffering. He called on the people, "Seek the LORD while he may be found," and then he spoke in the name of Yahweh:

"For my thoughts are not your thoughts,
Nor are my ways your ways," is the oracle of the LORD;
"But as the heavens are higher than the earth,
So are my ways higher than your ways,
And my thoughts than your thoughts."

(Isaiah 55:7-8, G)

## GOD'S POWER IN THE CROSS

God is love, and love is never helpless. God runs his world by means of an overruling providence. "God is working his purpose out." We make no mistake about this, for "God is not mocked." His love is revealed in the dependableness of his natural and moral law.

We see this most clearly in the Cross. The crucifixion shows us that Jesus Christ was subject to both the natural and the moral areas of God's law. Men who broke the moral law by crucifying an innocent man illustrated the consequences of sin in the face of goodness. But at the same time, Jesus was subject to natural law in that he died. He did not meet the demand for a miracle by coming down from the cross. In this acceptance of the consequences of law, Jesus revealed fully the love of God. "In this is love, not that we loved God, but that he loved us and sent his Son to be the expiation of our sins." (I John 4:10, RSV)

The power of God has always been the power of the Cross. It is the greatest power there is, for when one knows that God's power is established through love and through the death of Christ, one can bear any kind of suffering and evil. The Cross is God's power, telling us that God has an infinite capacity to endure any evil that men can do or suffer.

Our sins, not thine, thou bearest, Lord,
Make us thy sorrow feel,
Till through our pity and our shame
Love answers love's appeal.[2]

I know that God feels the pain and suffering and disaster that face every human being. He does not will our tragedy, but he suffers from it, just as he suffered when Jesus Christ was crucified. How can he bear it all? That is part of the mystery, but we know he can because he did. We pray,

Give me, for light, the sunshine of thy sorrow,
Give me, for shelter, the shadow of thy Cross;
Give me to share the glory of thy morrow,
Gone from my heart the bitterness of loss.[3]

### PROVIDENCE AND FREEDOM

Much of men's suffering is due to his freedom. Besides all that we suffer because of natural law, there is the suffering that results from the breaking of the moral law and from disobedience of God. In this loneliness of a willed separation from God, our suffering is more poignant than in the facing of natural tragedy. When we see the power of God's love in relation to freedom, we cease to be anxious about God's ultimate goodness.

D. R. Davies, in *Down Peacock Feathers,* puts it clearly: "What is love? Love is the power to grant freedom without desiring to limit or inhibit its exercise. It is the power to give freedom without any will to take it back. *And it is only omnipotence that can refrain absolutely from trespassing upon freedom.* Only God can give and not take back. . . . He suffers in Himself the entire consequences of allowing man absolute freedom. That is His love. It is also His omnipotence, which may be defined as the will and capacity to endure everything that man may inflict upon God through the exercise of his freedom. And that takes some doing!" [4]

This discovery of the meaning of God's love in relation to our freedom is the clue to maturity in the face of disaster due to moral causes. It is the answer to those who cry, "Why don't you force us to do your will?"

> He came as Saviour to his own,
> The way of love he trod;
> He came to win men by good will,
> For force is not of God.[5]

God works through men's freedom. Men who become his servants become also channels of his grace. Some men know that God works through them; others do not know it, but God works through them in his own way; and some men are opposed to God, but God works chiefly through those who love him. He worked through the saints of other times and he works through the saints of today. He works through significant people and insignificant people, as far as the judgments of secular society make men one or the other. In times of trouble, he inspires sympathy and affectionate companionship, and thus he comes to us through our friends and fellow believers. The resources of God are mediated through the love and understanding of our fellows, and this is what we mean by a redemptive and sustaining fellowship in the Church. God's grace heals our troubles as we turn to him in prayer, but prayer is often answered through the love given to us by other persons.

Chiefly, God worked in history through Jesus Christ, who lived and died and rose again for our justification. This impact of Jesus Christ on the world was not only the most important event in history, it is also the most important event in our lives today as the living Christ comes to us in prayer, worship, sacrament, and fellowship.

"Beloved, if God so loved us, we also ought to love one another. No man has ever seen God; if we love one another, God abides in us and his love is perfected in us." (I John 4:11-12, RSV)

## "NO FEAR IN LOVE"

"There is no fear in love, but perfect love casts out fear" (I John 4:18a, RSV). This is the great victory of religious maturity. It is never completely achieved, because we cannot maintain perfect love. But insofar as we love God who first loved us, we are freed from fear and anxiety. Our certainty of God's love is the basis for our lack of fear concerning our loved ones who are dead, for they are alive in Christ. We learn to accept the committal, "ashes to ashes, earth to earth, and dust to dust," in the "sure and certain hope of resurrection unto eternal life." "This is the testimony, that God gave us eternal life, and this life is in his Son. He who has the Son has life." (I John 5:11-12, RSV)

I remember how one courageous soul faced an operation with utmost confidence and without any fear at all, because she was able to sing the hymn of St. Patrick:

> Christ be with me, Christ within me,
> Christ behind me, Christ before me,
> Christ beside me, Christ to win me,
> Christ to comfort and restore me. . . .
> I bind unto myself today
> The strong Name of the Trinity.[6]

Finally, when all else fails, when failure must be faced, when tragedy is irrevocable, when death is final, there are the words of the Psalmist:

I will lift up mine eyes unto the hills; from whence cometh my
    help?
My help cometh even from the Lord, who hath made heaven and
    earth.
He will not suffer thy foot to be moved; and he that keepeth thee
    will not sleep.
Behold, he that keepeth Israel shall neither slumber nor sleep.
The Lord himself is thy keeper; the Lord is thy defence upon thy
    right hand;
So that the sun shall not burn thee by day, neither the moon by
    night.
The Lord shall preserve thee from all evil; yea, it is even thee that
    shall keep thy soul.
The Lord shall preserve thy going out, and thy coming in, from
    this time forth for evermore.          (Psalm 121, PB)

# PART VI

# THE PEACE OF GOD

# CHAPTER SEVENTEEN

# Anxiety or Christ

The heart of the answer to our basic fears and anxieties centers in faith in Jesus Christ. The focal point of a well-balanced Christian personality is faith in the living Christ, who was revealed in Jesus of Nazareth. There is a center of sanity in this kind of faith that comes as a gift of God.

There are anxious people who claim to believe in Christ. Being a nominal Christian is no guarantee against mental illness, and certain kinds of religious fanaticism may be either causes or symptoms of an underlying mental disturbance needing psychiatric care.

One of the reasons that people do not find freedom from anxiety through their faith is that this faith is wrongly oriented. They try to believe in Jesus the good man, or they have a mystical sense of a Christ who has no connection with the historic Jesus of Nazareth. They do not see the relationship between God's revelation of himself through the historical events recorded in the Bible and the religious demand on themselves today.

## *JESUS AS A GOOD MAN*

Let us look for a moment at Jesus as a good man. When this claim is made, the answer is that Jesus was a supremely good man. So was Gautama Buddha; so was Socrates; so was Francis of Assisi; so was Gandhi; so is Albert Schweitzer. As Christians we take Jesus as the prime example of what a man ought to be.

To begin with, there are the teachings of the Gospels that stand as a challenge to everyone seeking to live a good life. These are spelled out in some of the parables, in specific answers to direct questions, and in Paul's application of Jesus' sayings in the letters. Here is the guide to a moral and ethical life that modern Christians can adapt to the conditions of the twentieth century.

This ethical monotheism of Jesus is more than the urge to be good, however, for it is rooted in the belief that the God of our fathers will assist us if we turn to him. Our frustration as we find ourselves unable to achieve high moral standards is overcome as we discover that Jesus himself relied on the power of God in order to obey God. Our problem is how to gain access to this power, and it is the Christian faith that it comes through faith in Jesus as the Christ.

Jesus also stands as an example. He lived as a man who obeyed God. We are inspired by his teachings, but we find hope in the discovery that Jesus lived according to these standards. We do not seek to imitate his particular deeds or vocation, but we seek to be as obedient as he was. Here, again, there is frustration, because we discover that we cannot imitate him any better than we can obey his teachings. This despair accentuates our anxiety. Jesus had access to sources of power that we cannot imitate, and therefore our condition of anxiety becomes worse because our attempts to acquire this power end in failure. We cannot pull ourselves up to his level without help from outside ourselves.

This imitation of Jesus reaches the highest degree of confusion when we discover that the power given to Jesus resulted in miracles that we can neither understand nor duplicate. We may have reservations about the accuracy of some of the stories recounting the miracles, but the impact of the miracle stories as a whole leaves us with the impression that Jesus' compassion was such that people were healed through faith in him.

Jesus seen as a teacher and example is not adequate for mature Christian living today. A careful reading of the New Testament, however, fails to provide this picture of Jesus as simply a good man. The view of him as similar to Buddha or Socrates fails to account for the historical evidence, and it is actually a modern attempt to reconstruct the Gospel picture of Jesus in terms of naturalistic philosophy.

The earliest Gospel, Mark, is not the biography of a good man. It opens bluntly: "The beginning of the Gospel of Jesus Christ, the Son of God" (Mark 1:1, KJ). The writer of Mark cannot conceive of Jesus without adding the adjective "Christ," meaning "the anointed one." The prologue to the Gospel of John emphasizes that "the Word became flesh and dwelt among us" (John 1:14, KJ, RSV). Paul's letters and several sermons in Acts refer to Jesus, but they all consider Jesus as the center of their faith.

From the beginning it was the faith of the Church that Jesus was the Messiah, the Lord. Every creed in the history of Christendom makes the same startling claim, "I accept Jesus Christ as Lord and Savior." Every primitive Christian was a Jew, and yet Jews were baptized by the thousands. The earliest baptismal creed was simple and to the point: "I believe that

Jesus is the Christ." That was enough to mark off the Christian from his fellow Jews. To believe that Jesus was more than a teacher, more than a good man, more than a miracle worker, meant risking one's life as well as his orthodoxy. This was a "stumbling block" to all orthodox Jews and "foolishness" to the Greeks.

When non-Jews began to come into the Christian fold, it was necessary to expand the creed to say,

> I believe in God, the Father,
> In Jesus Christ, his only (or unique) Son,
> And in the Holy Spirit.

This was enough to cause a man to risk the ire of the emperor, to be thrown to the lions, to suffer in prison, to be burned at the stake. No one ever died for saying, "I believe that Jesus was a good man," but men and women throughout the ages have suffered for claiming that Jesus was the Christ, who died for men's sins and rose again for their justification.

## INCARNATION

Two technical words have been used to describe the Christian faith in Jesus Christ: Incarnation and Atonement. Incarnation means "in the flesh" and is derived from the statement in the Fourth Gospel that "the Word was made flesh and dwelt among us" (John 1:14, KJ, RSV).

"God so loved the world that he gave his only begotten Son, that whoever believes in him should not perish, but have eternal life" (John 3:16, RSV), is the way the Fourth Gospel describes it. Paul writes that "God was in Christ reconciling the world to himself" (II Corinthians 5:19). God was in Jesus Christ in a unique way. Jesus of Nazareth was completely human, but Christians believe that God dwelt in him fully and that, therefore, he is different from all other men who have ever lived. The total personality of Jesus is the channel by which God broke down the barrier set up by man and established a new and richer relationship with him.

This was not an easy doctrine to establish. Many devoted Christians came to the conclusion that Jesus only *seemed* to be a man and that in reality he was a deity in disguise. The later creed said that Jesus "became man" in order to refute the "seemists" or Docetists, and added that Jesus was born of a human mother, was tried before a real person named Pilate, died on the cross, and rose again. These instances were cited to show that Jesus was a man. We do not hear much of this early heresy today, but there are many Christians who forget that Jesus lived in a historical situation and who think of the Christ as an unhistorical and mystical figure.

The other heresy is that Jesus was a man and not divine in any unique sense. If we start with Jesus as a man, it is hard to conceive him as God incarnate. If we start with him as a God, it is difficult to see how he could be a man. It is a paradox, with only the hyphen in "God-man" to help us. In our attempts to work this out intellectually, we find that we have to hold both ideas. It is a mystery, and we cannot define it too carefully without destroying it. When we accept Jesus Christ as Lord and Saviour, we discover that he is "the way, the truth, and the life" (John 14:6, KJ), and we can pray, "let this mind be in you, which was also in Christ Jesus" (Philippians 2:5, KJ).

## ATONEMENT

The doctrine of the atonement tells us why God was in Christ. There was a reason for it. "For in Christ," says St. Paul, "God reconciled the world to himself" (II Corinthians 5:19,

M). Therefore, we say that God was in Christ (which is incarnation) because God wanted something done (which is atonement). By atonement, God changed the relationship between himself and man. The promise of salvation and eternal life comes from God through Christ.

The background for this claim is found in the Old Testament. It is the story of a covenant or agreement. It begins with Abraham and reaches a high point in the giving of the Ten Commandments to Moses. God is acting to redeem men and God remains faithful even when Israel fails to keep the law. In many ways, the Old Testament tells this story, and always there is hope that God will send a Messiah and bring in his kingdom. Jeremiah sees the law being written on men's hearts. Hosea tells of the need for suffering and forgiving love, for Israel as the bride of Yahweh has played the harlot and yet Yahweh will take the nation back. The Prophet of the exile, whom we call the second Isaiah (*see* Chapters 40-55), writes of a Suffering Servant who will take on himself the iniquities of all mankind. But there is pessimism, too, for "all is futility" (Ecclesiastes 1:2, G). The Old Testament sees Yahweh as forgiving and redemptive, willing to bring his people back into a right relationship with him, but the Messiah does not come.

The New Testament tells us not only that God cares enough, but also that God has entered the lists of history. He is willing to take the initiative, for he is the reconciler. The new covenant or agreement is written in blood, coming through the suffering love and the cruel death of Jesus of Nazareth. When Jesus gives the disciples the cup at the Last Supper, he says, "This is my blood which ratifies the agreement, and is to be poured out for many people" (Mark 14:24, G). This is the heart of the matter. When the disciples experience the presence of their Lord and Master after the resurrection, there is no doubt in their minds about what has happened. This final victory is the proof that this man is indeed the Messiah.

What happened after that is quite clear. Beginning among the earliest followers of Jesus, the new movement spread rapidly among the Jews first and then to the Gentiles. Their faith rested in the Resurrection, and it was a contagious faith. They remembered Jesus as he was, and they knew him as their risen Saviour. Out of this faith, by the guidance of the Holy Spirit, came the Christian Church.

The existence of the Church almost two thousand years later is a witness to the centrality of faith in Christ as the focal point of the Christian religion. Wherever men have believed in Jesus Christ, works have been done in his Name to make people whole. The Christian has this kind of faith in Jesus Christ. As a result, he develops a mature faith in which he finds poise and stability. He belongs to a community of faithful people and participates in its life, finding strength for living in the means of grace provided by the worship and sacraments of the Church. He knows that God loves him, although he is still a sinner. He knows that God has entered the arena of history in a unique way through Jesus Christ, and that God is continually present in that arena today as the Holy Spirit works through people.

Martin Luther emphasized that we are justified by faith and not by anything that we do. This justification is God's act, and it involves the restoring of our relationship with God. This new relationship is a fact of experience, by which we are forgiven of our sins and are treated as righteous. It turns on what Christ did for us. Charles R. Stinnette, Jr., stresses the historical realism of the Biblical story. "The event of Christ," he writes,

is of the stuff of history, and every forgiven sinner *lives into* that story by faith. This is no sentimental dream nor mystic's ecstatic vision. It happened in history; and the dust of Palestine, the sweat and grime of men's faces, the pain, the blood, and the exultant joy of it are attested by witnesses whose faith has touched the faith that touches ours.[1]

This new beginning that results from our faith and God's act is nurtured by the congregation of faithful people. The faithful person who is a new creature may still be a sinner, but the power of anxiety has been broken and men are set free to be obedient to God.

The New Testament knows no other religion than this. When we contrast the man-made creeds of faith in humanity, with its watered-down Jesus, against the power of the Gospel, it is terrifying to see the consequences. The Church at its best has always nurtured men in faith in Christ, and this has led to new life freed from anxiety and fear.[2]

## HOW TO FIND CHRIST

John Knox, in *Christ the Lord,* pictures the New Testament faith in Christ in three categories: he was remembered, he was known still, he was interpreted. When we first turn to search for Christ, we find him in the historical events recorded in Scripture. Here is the man Christ Jesus, who lived and died in a small corner of the earth some two thousand years ago. Every act of our seeking him today is in terms of the memory of the followers of Christ in the Christian community as they recorded their faith on the pages of what became the New Testament. We start with history, and we discover that we can understand the coming of Jesus Christ in terms of God's mighty acts.[3]

We share this memory of the Christian community through our membership in the Church. The Church re-enacts the Gospel story in its preaching and its worship, and always it comes to the Lord's Supper in memory of him who died for us. This is the starting point of Christian faith.

The disciples who remembered Christ knew him still. This is the miracle of the early Church. They did not belong to a society who remembered a dead hero. They belonged to a worshiping community that knew its Lord still. This is the discovery that takes us beyond the level of history and brings us to Christ as an eternal contemporary. This Jesus who was crucified and who is remembered is now known as the Christ of faith. By the power of the Holy Spirit he comes to us in our worship, and through faith in him we are justified and we find that our anxieties and loneliness and sins are overcome by the power of his forgiving love.

The disciples who remembered Jesus and knew him still as their Christ interpreted him. The New Testament is full of interpretations of how Jesus was the Christ. These answers ran all the way from how a man could become the Lord to how God could become a man. These explanations never stop, for we always must be able to give a reason for the faith that is in us. But once the Jesus who is remembered is seen in faith to be the Christ who is known still, we have arrived at the point of overcoming our anxieties. "By 'Christ,'" writes Knox,

we mean the One remembered and still known in the church, by whom we are grasped, through whom we are forgiven, in whom we have been found of God. By 'Christology' we mean the attempts of the church to explain this Reality. The two are closely related but are not identical. One can know Christ and 'the power of his resurrection' without finding entirely congenial any of the classical interpretations of that experience.[4]

When men know themselves as "heirs of God and fellow heirs with Christ" (Romans 8:17, RSV), their only question is, "How can I be loyal to him?" "Dear friends," wrote the Elder, "we

are God's children now; and it has not yet been disclosed what
we are to be. We know that if he appears, we shall be like him,
for we shall see him as he is. And everyone who possesses this
hope in him tries to make himself as pure as he is" (I John
3:2-3, G).

## THE MIND OF CHRIST [5]

When we know that we have faith in Christ and when our
state of anxiety has been overcome by God's grace, our thankful
response is to be worthy of our calling to serve God. Paul wrote,
"Let this mind be in you, which was also in Christ Jesus"
(Philippians 2:5, KJ). Archbishop William Temple put it this
way: "The truth of things is what they are in the mind of God,
and it is only when we act according to the mind of God that
we are acting in accordance with the truth, in accordance with
reality. Everything else is making a mistake." [6]

The various translations of Paul's phrase may prove helpful.
Moffatt translates, "Treat one another with the same spirit as
you experience in Christ Jesus." "Let Christ himself be your
example as to what your attitude should be," is Phillips' translation. Weymouth writes, "Let the same disposition be in you
which was in Christ Jesus." Goodspeed states it simply, "Have
the same attitude that Christ Jesus had."

Here is practical guidance from the teachings and example
of Jesus. We *do not start* with them as a means of earning salvation, but we *end* with them as our response to God's gracious
act in Christ whereby we are released from concern with ourselves. When we remember Christ, we share his mind, his spirit,
his example, his disposition, his attitude. When we know him
still as the risen Christ who comes to us by the power of the
Holy Spirit, we are empowered to know and do God's will.

But experience tells us that no one achieves perfection, and we know that only by God's grace are we ever justified.

In a remarkable passage in the Fourth Gospel, Jesus is recorded to have said, "If you continue in my word, you are my disciples, and you will know the truth, and the truth will make you free" (John 8:31b,32, RSV).

The truth that is in Jesus frees us from error, superstition, false ideals, and sin. We become reconciled to God, and therefore our anxieties are overcome. The love of God casts out our human fears.

Patrick Henry saw this in terms of freedom to achieve political goals when he cried out: "Is life so dear, or peace so sweet, as to be purchased at the price of chains and slavery? Forbid it, Almighty God! I know not what course others may take; but as for me, give me liberty or give me death!" Thomas Jefferson said it in a different way: "The God who gave us life, gave us liberty at the same time." Emile Zola believed that truth would always come through the darkness: "If you shut up truth and bury it underground, it will but grow, and gather to itself such explosive power that the day it bursts through, it will blow up everything in its way." It is the Christian conviction that

> Christ is the world's true light,
> Its captain of salvation,
> The Day-star clear and bright
> Of ev'ry man and nation.
> New life, new hope awakes,
> Whene'er men own his sway:
> Freedom her bondage breaks,
> And night is turned to day.[7]

During World War II, signs appeared everywhere among the troops of the Allied Nations saying, "Kilroy was here."

Robert Nelson Spencer took this thought and worked it into a Christmas poem.

'Kilroy was here,'
Yes, little scribbler,
No need to rub it in
With your small smidge of chalk
On every pave I walk—

Kilroy WAS here—here to win
For every little child
Freedom from fear!

You'll not forget
Kilroy was here?
And, when you're old enough,
Freedom from fear?

Child Jesus was here!
A star scribbled him
Blaze-glory across the sky,
Sprinkling us all with stardust;
So it is only just,
Now that his birth draws nigh,
To scribble on our very hearts:
'Child Jesus was here;
Here to bless us every one,
That none might ever fear.'

You'll not forget
Christ Jesus was here?
He planned it long before
Kilroy was here.[8]

The freedom that comes from having "the mind of Christ" transcends our political, social and religious freedoms. It is a freedom that can operate in the catacombs, that can persevere in the midst of persecution, and can raise its head in the most rigidly totalitarian society. It is a freedom that does not rely on law, that does not depend on the approval of one's neighbors, that does not equate itself with success in business. It is a freedom that overcomes anxiety because it centers in God who cannot be coerced by the powers of men. It reflects what Jesus said,

Have no fear of those who kill the body, but cannot kill the soul. You had better be afraid of one who can destroy both soul and body in the pit. Do not sparrows sell two for a cent? And yet not one of them can fall to the ground against your Father's will! But the very hairs on your heads are all counted. You must not be afraid; you are worth more than a great many sparrows! (Matthew 10:28-30, G)

"If God is for us, who is against us? He who did not spare his own Son but gave him up for us, will he not also give us all things with him? . . . For I am sure that neither death, nor life, . . . nor anything else in all creation, will be able to separate us from the love of God in Christ Jesus our Lord." (Romans 8:31-32,38,39, RSV)

# CHAPTER EIGHTEEN

# The Marvelous Peace of God

The reading habits of the people provide an index to the American mind, and it is a cause for rejoicing that religious books are among the best sellers. Many of these books are helpful as the people seek to find the answers to their basic concerns about the meaning of life.

Those who read these books want acceptance, security, and peace of mind, but often they want these gifts of God on what may be the wrong terms. They believe that by developing the right inner attitudes, by practicing the right mental exercises, by firm resolves of Stoic patience, and by being self-reliant, they can overcome their fears and anxieties, can stop worrying and start living.

Many readers of these books are asking the wrong questions. They ask, "How can *I* get what I want from God? What good will church-going do *me?* How can *I* find peace of mind?" When Jesus looked at such goals among the people of his day, he said,

Never think I have come to bring peace upon the earth. No, I have not come to bring peace but a sword! . . . Anyone who puts his love for father or mother above his love for me does not deserve to be mine, and he who loves son or daughter more than me is not worthy of me, and neither is the man who refuses to take up his cross and follow my way. The man who has found his own life will lose it, but the man who has thrown it away for my sake will find it. (Matthew 10:34,37-39, P)

What Jesus is saying is that no man ever found happiness by seeking it; all he finds is momentary pleasure. No man ever found peace of mind by making it his chief goal; all he ever finds is appeasement involving an insensitivity to the sufferings and needs of others. No man ever escaped from the trials and tribulations of the world by withdrawal; all he finds is the solitary life of a hermit or the psychological solitariness of a mental hospital. Only when a man is caught up in a great cause or a great loyalty or a great faith does he find a peace that he never sought and that passes man's understanding.

### WHAT IS THE PEACE OF GOD?

William Alexander Percy caught the spirit of Biblical peace when he wrote:

> They cast their nets in Galilee
> Just off the hills of brown;
> Such happy, simple fisherfolk,
> Before the Lord came down.[1]

This kind of happiness depends on the regularity of the fish, the stability of the fishermen's homes, and the good health of their families. These are goods in themselves and much to be desired, but they do not provide the kind of integration of personality that guarantees true peace in the midst of the tensions and conflicts and sufferings of life. These men were willing to leave their jobs and homes, with which they were contented, because they were challenged by a great prophet who became their Master.

Contented, peaceful fishermen,
Before they ever knew
The peace of God that filled their hearts
Brimful, and broke them too.

The Gospel of Jesus Christ is an uncomfortable kind of good news, for it contradicts the impulses of pleasure-loving and self-seeking men. It says, in effect, that you cannot buy your way into heaven. The only peace that comes to you is a side issue, coming as a gift of God when you have sought to place yourself in his hands.

What Jesus demands is an uncompromising loyalty that seems shocking at first. You are to love him more than you love those to whom you are bound by blood. You are to love him so much that you forget about yourself. You are to accept the cross of costly grace. Jesus never promised more than this. He said,

Men will deliver you up to the courts,
And they will scourge you in their synagogues,
And you will be brought before governors and kings,
To testify to them and to the heathen.

(Matthew 10:17-18, E)

Jesus accepted no excuses, even when it was as important as saying "good-bye" to your family or burying your dead. He promised nothing except trouble, and that is what his disciples faced.

Young John, who trimmed the flapping sail,
Homeless, in Patmos died.
Peter, who hailed the teeming net,
Head-down was crucified.

There is no record of any of the disciples dying in bed. In early days, Christians were social outcasts, ended up in jail, and were fed to the lions. They were isolated and ignored in some communities, and were taunted and stoned in others. They held no political offices, received no preferment in their work, and often lived in places of hiding.

Contrast this Gospel of Jesus Christ with the modern seekers after peace of mind or soul, looking for relief by reading the right books and taking proper spiritual exercises. They want security without struggle, salvation without a price, serenity without pain. Too often their religion is like that described by H. Richard Niebuhr: "A God without wrath brought men without sin into a kingdom without judgment through the ministrations of a Christ without a cross." [2]

The Gospel provides good news, all right, but it is strikingly different in kind from the modern cult of peace of mind. The "peace that passes understanding" provides a sense of blessedness and joy even in the midst of sorrow and suffering, because Christian joy has the dimension of eternal life. "Where there is joy," writes Paul Tillich, "there is fulfillment. And where there is fulfillment, there is joy. In fulfillment and joy the inner aim of life, the meaning of creation, and the end of salvation, are attained." [3]

> The peace of God, it is no peace,
> But strife closed in the sod.
> Yet, brothers, pray for but one thing—
> The marvelous peace of God.

This is what the Fourth Gospel was talking about when Jesus said, "Peace I leave with you; my peace I give to you; not as the world gives do I give to you. Let not your hearts be troubled, neither let them be afraid" (John 14:27, RSV).

Peace is something *given,* not something that you achieve. You do not get it by playing any tricks or making adjustments within yourself, or by revising your concept of values. You may pray for it, but you cannot earn it. The chief thing to do is to *forget about it,* but you can do this only when you *"accept the fact that you are accepted."* [4] The trouble with all of your efforts to raise yourself by your bootstraps is just this: no one can give you the peace that passes understanding except God himself, and it comes only when you turn from considering yourself and place God at the center of your life.

## GRACE AND FAITH

The writer of the letter to the Ephesians tells us that "by grace you have been saved through faith; and this is not your own doing, it is the gift of God—not because of works, lest any man should boast. For we are his workmanship, created in Christ Jesus for good works, which God prepared beforehand, that we should walk in them" (Ephesians 2:8-10, RSV). Apart from this assurance of God's gift of grace, the burdens of life are intolerable. This grace of God provides forgiveness, restoration to fellowship with man and God, and the power to be worthy of our vocations.

We are drawn into a holy fellowship centered in Christ, and in this community of the Holy Spirit we know redemption.

For Christ is our living Peace. He has made a unity of the conflicting elements of Jew and Gentile by breaking down the barrier which lay between us. By His sacrifice He removed the hostility of the Law, with all its commandments and rules, and made in Himself out of the two, Jew and Gentile, One New Man, thus producing peace. For He reconciled both to God by the sacrifice of one Body on the Cross, and by this act made utterly irrelevant the antagonism between them. Then He came and told, both you who were far from God and us who were near, that the war was over. And it is through Him that both of us now can approach the Father in one Spirit.

So you are no longer outsiders or aliens, but fellow-citizens with every other Christian—you belong now to the household of God. (Ephesians 2:14-19, P)

There is a dynamic peace in this faith, because it eliminates concern for the self from the center of the picture. It is an out-going faith and shows its fruits in courageous and daring living. The serenity and maturity and peace of mind that result are accompanying gifts, but they cease to be the center of the soul's desire.

We see that the search for peace of mind is self-defeating. Just as worry does not add to a man's span of life, but actually shortens it, so anxiety about peace of mind accentuates the state of anxiety. There are no tricks that solve the problem. There is no way to manufacture anxiety-free periods, even in sleep. Peace of mind becomes a will o' the wisp whenever we directly seek it.

Only when God is your confidence and your strength, when you put first things first, when you "seek first his kingdom and his righteousness," shall "all these things . . . be yours as well" (Matthew 6:33, RSV). "Man," said the bishops at the Lambeth Conference of 1948, "is a being created by God and is under his sovereignty, and . . . apart from God, he can neither master his nature nor find his true self."


## PEACE, COURAGE, AND JOY

The call to every man is to follow Christ. As we remember him, know him still, and interpret him within the community of faithful people, we find that our basic needs are met, our deepest questions about the meaning of life are answered, and our ultimate concern as a creature of the holy Creator is satisfied through discipleship.

> If any man would be my disciple,
> Let him deny himself;

And so let him follow me.

(Mark 8:34, E)

It is not an easy way, for it takes everything a man has. It means keeping at the task and staying on the way.

Enter in by the narrow gate!
For wide is the gate and broad the way that leads to destruction,
 And many there are who are entering it;
For narrow is the gate and strait the way that leads to life,
 And few there are who are finding it.   (Matthew 7:13-14, E)

When a man has a vision of the kingdom of God, he is like "a merchant in search of pearls; who having found one pearl of great price, went and sold all that he had, and bought it" (Matthew 13:45-46, E).

Belief in God is not enough. "You believe that God is one; you do well. Even the demons believe—and shudder." (James 2:19, RSV) We are not saved by what we believe or by what we know or by what we do. We are saved by faith, and faith is commitment of the total self, a joyous giving of ourselves in trust to the living God, an entering into a new and transformed relationship with a God of grace. It is also a commitment on our part of all whom we love to God's care, knowing that he is doing for them more than we can desire or pray for. The result is not peace at all in the worldly sense.

The peace of God, it is no peace,
But strife closed in the sod.

When Jesus said, "Be not anxious," he was opening the way to all the glories of the Gospel. To be free from worries and fretfulness and concerns is to be on the road to salvation. To overcome our loneliness and frustration and separation and sin is to know God's personal gift of grace as we are forgiven and restored to fellowship with God and with our fellow men.

Paul wrote of peace and always combined it with joy. "So may God, the fountain of hope, fill you with all joy and peace in your believing, so that you may enjoy overflowing hope by the power of the Holy Spirit." (Romans 15:13, VK)

The result is the joyous service of the Lord and Master in all that we do, coming to him in faith and using our hearts and souls and minds to serve and love him. Our vocation is our witness to him in every act, taking us out of ourselves as we bring the healing gifts of God to families, friends, neighbors, and the community. Our vocation involves us in political action and moral reform, in good business relationships and interest in people as ends in themselves.

The promise of eternal life stands as a present gift, offered to you *now,* not postponed to the after life. The "life abundant" promised by Christ is yours *now,* and the gifts of God's grace shower down upon you and you have all the rejoicing that comes from a full and meaningful life.

Paul said it:

Rejoice in the Lord always; again I say, Rejoice. Let all men know your forbearance. The Lord is at hand. Have no anxiety about anything, but in everything by prayer and supplication with thanksgiving let your requests be made known to God. And the peace of God, which passes all understanding, will keep your hearts and your minds in Christ Jesus. (Philippians 4:4-7, RSV)

Yet, brothers, pray for but one thing—
The marvelous peace of God.

# NOTES

CHAPTER ONE: BE NOT ANXIOUS

1. John W. Suter, Jr., *Prayers of the Spirit* (New York: Harper & Bros., 1943), pp. 27-28. Used by permission of the publisher.

2. *The Best of Studdert-Kennedy* (New York: Harper & Bros., 1948), p. 91. Used by permission of the publisher.

CHAPTER TWO: THE OUTSIDE WORLD

1. Both prayers are found in *The Book of Common Prayer,* p. 597.

2. *See* Rollo May, *The Meaning of Anxiety* (New York: Ronald Press Company, 1950), pp. 334-44.

3. Paul Tillich, *The Protestant Era* (University of Chicago Press, 1948), p. 245. Copyright 1948 by the University of Chicago and used by permission.

4. *Ibid.,* p. 247.

5. Gerhardt Tersteegen, translated by Henry Sloane Coffin, from *The Hymnal 1940,* No. 477 (New York: Church Pension Fund, 1943). Used by permission of Mrs. Henry Sloane Coffin.

6. Anonymous, 1878. First appearance in *Pilgrim Hymnal* of 1904.

7. A technical treatment of Paul Tillich's approach to anxiety and belief in God is found in *Systematic Theology* (Chicago: University of Chicago Press, 1951), I, 191-201, 252-289.

CHAPTER THREE: SINMOBILE

1. December, 1946. Reprinted in Evans, *The Spoor of Spooks and Other Nonsense* (New York: Alfred A. Knopf, 1954), pp. 183-86. Used by permission of the author.

2. From *A Missionary Service Book,* 1937. See *The Hymnal 1940* (New York: The Church Pension Fund, 1943), No. 513, stanza 2. Used by permission of the publisher.

CHAPTER FOUR: BARRIERS TO CHRISTIAN LIVING

1. The quoted words are from the following versions respectively: VK, W, M, and KJ.

2. G (M also), W, K, and B.

3. G (W also), M, KJ, 20, and K.

4. G (M, VK also), KJ, W, 20, and K.

5. Walter Russell Bowie. *The Hymnal 1940,* No. 494, stanza 3. Used by permission of Harper & Bros.

CHAPTER FIVE: THE EVIL THAT GOODNESS DOES

1. James Luther Adams, *Voices of Liberalism* (Boston: Beacon Press, 1948), II, 61. Used by permission of the publisher.

2. *Voices of Liberalism,* II, 64.

3. F. Bland Tucker. *The Hymnal 1940* (New York: Church Pension Fund, 1943), No. 298, paraphrasing the "Address to Diognetus." Used by permission of F. Bland Tucker and the publisher.

4. "The Address to Diognetus," 5:1-2,5,6-7,10-11,13,17; 6:1, in *The Apostolic Fathers; An American Translation,* by Edgar J. Goodspeed (New York: Harper & Bros., 1950), p. 278. Used by permission of the publisher.

CHAPTER SIX: ANXIETY AND APPLE PIE

1. *See* Martin Buber, *Between Man and Man* (London: Routledge & Kegan Paul, 1947), pp. 83-117.

2. Walter Russell Bowie. *The Hymnal 1940,* No. 522. Used by permission of Abingdon Press.

CHAPTER SEVEN: WHAT TENSIONS ARE FOR

1. Robinson Jeffers, *Thurso's Landing* (New York: Random House). Used by permission of the publisher.

2. Quoted by Halford Luccock, *Christianity and the Individual in a World of Crowds* (Nashville: Abingdon-Cokesbury Press, 1937), p. 92. Used by permission of the publisher.

3. See *The Lonely Crowd,* by David Riesman, Nathan Glazer, Reuel Denny, abridged edition (New York: Doubleday & Co., 1954), pp. 34-38.

4. Samuel Hoffenstein, *Poems in Praise of Practically Nothing* (New York: Boni and Liveright, 1928). Used by permission of Liveright Publishing Corporation.

5. Hartley Burr Alexander, *Odes and Lyrics* (Boston: Marshall Jones Co., 1922), p. 9. Used by permission of Hubert Alexander.

CHAPTER EIGHT: GREAT CHRISTIANS ARE MADE

1. *See* Floyd V. Filson, *Pioneers of the Primitive Church* (New York: The Abingdon Press, 1940), pp. 83-113.

2. Albert Schweitzer, *Bach* (New York: The Macmillan Co., 1950), I, 169-70. Used by permission of the publisher.

3. Quoted by Schweitzer in *Bach,* I, 257-58.

4. From *A Compend of Luther's Theology,* edited by Hugh Thompson Kerr, Jr., p. 116 (Copyright 1943, by The Westminster Press, Philadelphia). Used by permission of the publisher.

5. *Religion in Life,* Summer 1942, p. 494. Used by permission of the publisher.

6. Quoted in *William Temple, Archbishop of Canterbury: His Life and His Letters,* by F. A. Iremonger (London: Oxford University Press, 1948), pp. 134-35. Used by permission of the publisher.

7. *The Church Looks Forward* (New York: The Macmillan Co., 1945), p. 2. Used by permission of the publisher.

8. Charles Lowry, *Christendom,* Winter 1943, p. 41. Used by permission.

9. *The Church Looks Forward,* p. 193.

10. Arnold Toynbee, *The Study of History,* abridged edition

(New York: Oxford University Press, 1946), p. 129. Used by permission of the publisher.

11. Lesbia Scott. *The Hymnal 1940* (New York: Church Pension Fund, 1943), No. 243. Copyright by Morehouse-Gorham Co. and used by permission.

CHAPTER NINE: THE LARK IS IN THE SKY

1. G. A. Studdert-Kennedy, *The Unutterable Beauty* (London: Hodder & Stoughton, Ltd., 1927), p. 135. Used by permission of the publisher.

2. *The Unutterable Beauty*, p. 75; *The Hymnal 1940*, No. 156.

3. *The Unutterable Beauty*, p. 110.

4. *The Unutterable Beauty*, p. 95.

5. *The Unutterable Beauty*, p. 75.

6. Quoted by Wade Crawford Barclay, *Challenge and Power*, p. 43. Used by permission of the publisher.

7. William Temple, in *The Best of Studdert-Kennedy* (New York: Harper & Bros., 1948), pp. 5-6. Italics mine. Used by permission of the publisher.

8. Erica Oxenham, *Scrap-Book of J.O.* (New York: Longmans, Green & Co., 1946), p. 25. Used by permission of Erica Oxenham.

9. From *Gentlemen—the King. The Hymnal 1940*, No. 510, stanza 4. Used by permission of Erica Oxenham.

10. *Scrap-Book of J.O.*, pp. 60-61.

11. *Scrap-Book of J.O.*, p. 65.

12. From *Bees in Amber.* See *The Hymnal 1940*, No. 263. Used by permission of Erica Oxenham.

13. *See* Robert M. Bartlett, *They Dare to Believe* (New York: Association Press, 1952), pp. 112-118, for a fuller story of Madeleine Barot.

14. Daniel Day Williams, *God's Grace and Man's Hope* (New York: Harper & Bros., 1949), p. 147. Italics his. Used by permission of the publisher.

15. *See* Alexander Miller, "Towards a Doctrine of Vocation," in *Christian Faith and Social Action,* ed. John A. Hutchison (New York: Charles Scribner's Sons, 1953), p. 134.

16. *See* Robert L. Calhoun, "Work as a Christian Vocation

Today," in *Work and Vocation,* ed. John Oliver Nelson (New York: Harper & Bros., 1954), pp. 171-177.

### CHAPTER TEN: A VIGOROUS AND VITAL FAITH

1. "Martyrdom of Polycarp," 8:2—10:1, 11:2—12:2, in Edgar J. Goodspeed, *The Apostolic Fathers* (New York: Harper & Bros., 1950), pp. 250-252. Used by permission of the publisher.

2. Dietrich Bonhoeffer, *The Cost of Discipleship* (New York: The Macmillan Co., 1948), pp. 37-39. See pp. 7-33 for a brief story of his life. Used by permission of the publisher.

3. "Martyrdom of Polycarp," 13:3, in Edgar J. Goodspeed, *The Apostolic Fathers,* p. 252. Used by permission of the publisher.

4. *Book of Common Prayer,* p. 258.

### CHAPTER ELEVEN: THE JOY OF BELIEVING

1. *See* Edgar J. Goodspeed, *The Life of Jesus* (New York: Harper & Bros., 1950), pp. 37, 46, 87.

2. C. C. McCown, *The Search for the Real Jesus* (New York: Charles Scribner's Sons, 1940), p. 163. Used by permission of the publisher.

3. Burton Scott Easton, *What Jesus Taught* (Nashville: Abingdon-Cokesbury Press, 1938), p. 87. Used by permission.

4. G. K. Chesterton, *Songs of Praise* (London: Oxford University Press), No. 308. *The Hymnal 1940,* No. 521. Used by permission of the publisher.

### CHAPTER TWELVE: LIFT UP YOUR HEARTS

1. Quoted by Leon and Elfrieda McCauley, *The Book of Prayers* (New York: Dell Publishing Co., 1954), p. 65. Used by permission of Reinhold Niebuhr.

2. From "The Eternal Goodness," *The Poetical Works of John Greenleaf Whittier* (Boston: James Osgood & Co., 1867), p. 389.

3. *See* Charles F. Whiston, *Teach Us to Pray* (Boston: Pilgrim Press, 1949), pp. 81-82.

4. Mrs. J. C. Simpson and others, *Songs of Praise* (London: Oxford University Press, 1931), No. 629. Used by permission of the publisher.

5. Edmund Vance Cooke, "Prayer," *The Uncommon Commoner* (New York: Dodge Publishing Co., 1913).

6. See *Interpreter's Bible*, VIII, 202-205.

7. In *Songs of Praise* (London: Oxford University Press, 1931), No. 565; *The Hymnal 1940*, No. 363. Used by permission of the publisher.

CHAPTER THIRTEEN: THE REFRESHMENT OF CHRISTIAN WORSHIP .

1. James Bissett Pratt, *Eternal Values in Religion* (New York: The Macmillan Co., 1950), p. 4. Used by permission of the publisher.

2. T. S. Eliot, "Choruses from the Rock," *The Complete Poems and Plays* (New York: Harcourt, Brace & Co., 1952), pp. 97-98. Used by permission of the publisher.

3. *Eternal Values in Religion*, p. 73.

4. William Temple, *Hope of a New World*, p. 30; quoted in *Daily Readings from William Temple* (London: Hodder and Stoughton, 1950), No. 13. Used by permission of the publisher.

5. *The Hymnal 1940*, No. 405.

6. Charles R. Stinnette, Jr., *Anxiety and Faith* (Greenwich: Seabury Press, 1955), pp. 193-94. Used by permission of the publisher.

7. George Wallace Briggs, in *Songs of Praise* (London: Oxford University Press, 1931), No. 266; *The Hymnal 1940*, No. 207. Used by permission of the publisher.

8. From *The Public Worship of God*, by Henry Sloane Coffin, pp. 141, 142, 144 (Copyright, 1946, by The Westminster Press). Used by permission of the publisher.

9. *The Hymnal 1940*, No. 190.

10. From *A Compend of Luther's Theology*, edited by Hugh Thomson Kerr, Jr., pp. 170-171 (copyright, 1943, by The Westminster Press). Used by permission of the publisher.

CHAPTER FOURTEEN: HOW THE CHURCH HELPS

1. From *Anxiety in Christian Experience*, by Wayne E. Oates, p. 153 (Copyright, 1955, by W. L. Jenkins, The Westminster Press). Used by permission of the publisher.

2. From *Bees in Amber*. Used by permission of Erica Oxenham.

3. See *You Need the Church* (Cincinnati: Forward Movement Publications); also my *Education for Christian Living* (Englewood Cliffs, N. J.: Prentice-Hall, Inc., 1956), pp. 139-146.

CHAPTER FIFTEEN: WHEN LIFE SEEMS HARD

1. John Bunyan, in *Songs of Praise* (London: Oxford University Press, 1931); also, *The Hymnal 1940*, No. 563. Used by permission of the publisher.

2. H. W. Dresser, *Voices of Freedom*, p. 38. Quoted by William James, *The Varieties of Religious Experience* (New York: Longmans, Green & Co., 1902), p. 99. Used by permission of the publisher.

3. *The Hymnal 1940*, No. 564, stanza 2. Used by permission of the publisher.

4. See *Of Things Not Seen*, by Harriet H. Houser (New York: The Macmillan Co., 1955).

5. Evelyn Atwater Cummins, in *The Hymnal 1940*, No. 432. Used by permission of the author.

CHAPTER SIXTEEN: FACING THE INEVITABLE

1. *The Hymnal 1940* (New York: The Church Pension Fund, 1943), No. 477. Used by permission of Dorothy Prentice Coffin.

2. Peter Abelard, translated by F. Bland Tucker, in *The Hymnal 1940* (New York: Church Pension Fund, 1943), No. 68, stanza 2. Used by permission of F. Bland Tucker and the publisher.

3. G. A. Studdert-Kennedy, *The Unutterable Beauty* (London: Hodder & Stoughton, 1927), p. 4. Used by permission of the publisher.

4. D. R. Davies, *Down Peacock Feathers* (New York: The Macmillan Co., 1944), p. 23. Used by permission of the publisher.

5. From "Address to Diognetus," translated by F. Bland Tucker, *The Hymnal 1940*, No. 298, stanza 5. Used by permission of F. Bland Tucker and the publisher.

6. *The Hymnal 1940*, No. 268, stanzas 6, 7. Used by permission of the publisher.

CHAPTER SEVENTEEN: ANXIETY OR CHRIST

1. Charles R. Stinnette, Jr., *Anxiety and Faith* (Greenwich: Seabury Press, 1955), p. 121. Used by permission of the publisher.

2. See my *The Clue to Christian Education* (New York: Charles Scribner's Sons, 1950), pp. 18-28.

3. See my *Biblical Theology and Christian Education* (New York: Charles Scribner's Sons, 1956); also my *A Symphony of the Christian Year* (Greenwich: Seabury Press, 1954), pp. 12-18.

4. John Knox, *Christ the Lord* (New York: Harper & Brothers, 1945), p. 121. Used by permission of the publisher.

5. See my *A Symphony of the Christian Year*, pp. 213-219.

6. William Temple, *Basic Convictions* (New York: The Macmillan Co.), p. 78. Used by permission of the publisher.

7. George Wallace Briggs, from *Songs of Praise* (London: Oxford University Press, 1931), No. 60. See *Hymnal 1940*, No. 258.

8. *Kansas City Star,* 1947. Used by permission of the author.

CHAPTER EIGHTEEN: THE MARVELOUS PEACE OF GOD

1. From *Enzio's Kingdom and Other Poems* by William Alexander Percy (New Haven: Yale University Press, 1924); see *The Hymnal 1940,* No. 437. Used by permission of the publisher and Mr. LeRoy Pratt Percy.

2. H. Richard Niebuhr, *The Kingdom of God in America* (New York: Harper & Brothers, 1937), p. 193. Used by permission of the publisher.

3. Paul Tillich, *The New Being* (New York: Charles Scribner's Sons, 1955), p. 151. Used by permission of the publisher.

4. Paul Tillich, *The Shaking of the Foundations* (New York: Charles Scribner's Sons, 1948), p. 162. Used by permission of the publisher.

# INDEX

# Index

(The more important topics are listed with pages in *italic* type.)

# BIBLICAL REFERENCES

# Biblical References

## OLD TESTAMENT

## NEW TESTAMENT

222-257-C-7.5